BUZZ BOMB

Diary

Compiled by
D. G. COLLYER

KAHRS

KENT AVIATION HISTORICAL RESEARCH SOCIETY

Published in Great Britain by
Kent Aviation Historical Research Society
25 Pilot's Avenue,
DEAL,
Kent,
CT14 9HQ

ISBN 0-9507408-1-0

British Library Cataloguing in Publication Data.
A catalogue record for this book is available from the British Library.

Computer set by
ARIOMA Editorial Services,
Gloucester House, High Street,
BORTH, Dyfed. SY24 5HZ

Printed by
Cambrian Printers,
22 Queen Street,
ABERYSTWYTH,
Dyfed,
SY23 1PX

Cover picture by Sam Mickwee

CONTENTS

INTRODUCTION

'Kent and the campaign against the V weapons'

Flying Officer G.G. Baxter R.A.F. (Intelligence) Retd.

The existence of the V-1 flying bomb had been known early in 1943 as a result of photographic reconnaissance flown by both the R.A.F and U.S.A.A.F, and supported by intelligence from the underground movement in Europe. This was finally proved beyond doubt when the Polish secret army recovered warheads, and shipped them out on a Dakota through Bari in Italy. By 23rd April 1944 it had been established that these Flying Bombs were about to become operational.

With a view to being able to provide some public early warning the radars at Swingate (Dover), Rye, Pevensey and Poling in No 11 Group RAF area had been modified. Later the Army set up gun operations rooms, including ones at Dover Castle and Chatham. Later still the Chain Home Low radar at South Foreland, Foreness and Whitstable were modified, and Sandwich was given a missile early warning facility. All the information from these sources was filtered by No 11 Group headquarters.

In an effort to delay and even reduce the launching of the V-1's, offensive strikes were carried out, the majority from Kent airfields. From April No 11 group were to ensure that at least two day fighters were on armed reconnaissance patrols over the rocket storage areas and the logistical routes to them. At night similar sorties were flown by intruder aircraft and to carry out this task, six Mosquito Mk IX's were stationed, three at Manston and three at Hunsdon (Norfolk), and kept at 30 minutes readiness. The nature of the sites was such that they could only be attacked using new techniques. These were taught to pilots on a dummy site in Wales.

In addition to the above tactics both R.A.F Bomber Command and the U.S. 8th Air Force heavy bombers made large scale attacks on the more concentrated targets. As a result of all these efforts it was possible to launch the 'D-Day' invasion on 6th June 1944, before a V-1's attack could interfere. The first launching of a V-1 was on 13th June, crossing the Kent coast near Dymchurch exploding 12 minutes later in a wood at Swanscombe near Gravesend.

By August the anti-aircraft defences, reduced owing to the War Office considering that Luftwaffe resistance was practically finished, were soon overwhelmed by '24 hour' watches that additional crews had to be rushed in from other divisions. The initial defences involved fighters patrolling off the coast and chasing V-1's inland, which entailed the crossing of anti-aircraft batteries, leading to losses to 'friendly fire'. Thus, by mid-August, a revision of tactics evolved designated zones being set up incorporating a coastal 'gun belt' from Littlehampton to North Foreland which fighters were prohibited to cross, taking over inland between the coast and a barrage balloon belt around the outskirts of London. For the R.A.F, a peak was reached in August when 15 day and 10 night fighter squadrons were averaging 102 successes a day. It was quickly realised that flying bombs were being air launched when attacks were made against Southampton, Hull, Gloucester and Manchester by Heinkel He 111H-5s of KG53, with specially trained crews, carrying one or two V-1's slung under the wings. The bomb aimer had a special instrument panel with controls to start or stop the missile's motors and a lever which released them. Great secrecy surrounded these operations, crews being billeted five miles away from their airfields, and only allowed on the airfield in darkness before flying. By the time the operation finished this unit had launched some 1200 bombs, but had suffered high casualties as a result of night fighter interceptions. As the Pas de Calais sites were overrun by the Allies the launching areas were moved northwards and the defences were gradually transferred to East Anglia.

Some scores of Kent based squadrons

No 3	Squadron	Tempest F.5	Newchurch	275
No 486	Squadron	"	"	241
No 322	Squadron	Spitfire XIV	West Malling	108
No 129	Squadron	Mustang III	Brenzett	66

BUZZ BOMB DIARY

This is not a book specifically about the V-1, the R.A.F.'s efforts to shoot them down, nor the anti-aircraft or balloon defences, but it is a record of reported incidents by area linked to reminiscences of a wide selection of those who either lived or served in the county of Kent during June - August 1944. The lists of incidents have been made from A.R.P. records and may be incomplete, due to the intensive attacks in the initial period or the subsequent loss of records, however it is hoped that readers will be able to discover if, or when a 'Buzz Bomb' landed in their particular village or town.

We have included the former Kent boroughs and parishes, which were later absorbed by the L.C.C., as the majority of the 'Men of Kent' and 'Kentish Men'(and women) still regard them as being within our county. From the listing of incidents it is possible to gauge the success of the defences against the V-1 during the latter part of the assault and the number of incidents, especially in the London boroughs, falls-off significantly during August, apart from those involving air-launched V-1's. No attempt has been made to cover the V- 2 rockets but some of these incidents are mentioned in passing.

We have tried to cover all aspects of the defences, including the naval personnel who were involved, both at sea and ashore, as well as those serving in both R.A.F and the U.S.A.A.F who were instrumental in intercepting these missiles. Every kind of anti-aircraft device, even including Z-battery rockets were used, and at many Heavy Ack-Ack sites the A.T.S. girls worked alongside their male counterparts. Memories of schoolboys and girls who grew up during this time (as I did) include a selection of personal involvement when houses or schools were hit, and some humorous anecdotes are mixed with those tragedies which occurred when many casualties were involved.

Some of the illustrations may be familiar to those who have read the books compiled by the late H.R. Pratt-Boorman, former owner of the 'Kent Messenger' newspaper, but we have tired to select photographs of those whose reminiscences have been used, as well as those representative of all aspects of the defences, many of which have not been seen previously. Also included is a section dealing with Radar and ack-ack with appropriate illustrations, and the individual maps at the start of each section are included to assist those who are searching for any particular incident in their local area.

The response to our appeal for reminiscences for *Buzz Bomb Diary* was overwhelming in some areas, and many fascinating accounts have had to be omitted due to lack of space. However I hope that this book will give a flavour of what it was like to be living under attack by a missile which announced its arrival with a distinctive sound that will never be forgotten by those who heard it, listening intently for it to stop, and diving for the nearest shelter when the motor cut out.

David. G. Collyer
Archivist K.A.H.R.S
Project Co-ordinator
January 1994

ACKNOWLEDGEMENTS

This book has been a co-operative effort by the members of the Kent Aviation Historical Research Society, but special thanks are due to the following :-

Mr Geoff Baxter;	Mr Paul Grundy;	Mrs Sue Grundy:	Mr Roy Humphreys;
Mr Bob McNae;	Mr Tony Moor;	Mr Ray Munday;	Mr Len Pilkington;
Mr Ken Owen;	Mr Ted Sergison;	Mr John Williams;	Mr Alan Wright.

BUT MOST OF ALL TO OUR CORRESPONDENTS WHO HAVE SHARED THEIR REMINISCENCES OF THE BUZZ BOMBS WITH US, AND YOU!

Cover Picture

Hitler's secret weapon, dubbed the 'Doodle Bug' by Pilots, is shown in flight over our base at Ashford, Kent, England, on its way to London. Two Typhoons are shown about to intercept the projectile, which is travelling at approximately 350 miles per hour. They often flew through flak thrown up by anti-aircraft batteries. Many doodle bugs were shot down before reaching London, many landing near our base. We were forced to take shelter in our fox holes when the Doodle Bug passed over our base, as following flak was extremely heavy, besides we never knew when the engine would quit and the flying bomb would crash earthward. They hit and exploded with a tremendous blast.

Sam Mickwee.

ODE TO THE DOODLE BUG

by R.H SAUTER of Wittersham, Kent. 27th July 1944

Stands Wittersham still,
Looking over to France,
Beneath the Flying Bomb
On the nape of the hill ?
Stands Wittersham where
This morning she stood
When I rose and set out
And departed from there ?
For the hunt was up at the break of day
Over Sussex and Kent towards London way,
Where the evil black fox goes streaking away
To the sound of the Siren's warning.

Is the house still cream
And rufous and grey ?
Still crinkled the roof
And weathered the beam ?
With a friendly gleam
In the ancient eye
For the many things
which so lovely seem ?
For I've seen the whole pack of them hunting at noon
Spitfire, Mosquito - Mustang, Typhoon;
Tempest and Thunderbolt, hot to the tune
And the baying of the guns in the morning.

Oh I would learn
If my Love be safe,
If my Love be safe
Till my return -
And the home there, still
And sanctuary
At journey's end
On Oxney hill
For I have known the snarl and the bite
The sudden quiet and the twisting flight
And the glare and the bang and the kill - and the sight
Of the plume of smoke on that Kentish hill.

Stands Wittersham, still
In the rose-drunk dusk ?
And the evening owl
On the mill - on the mill ?
Where peace resides
In the open door,
Is all then well
Where my Loved one bides ?
For the chase will be on with the fall of night
When the Doodle-bug flickers his sinister light
In the horns of the searchlights, and the tracer is bright
From the view to the blast and the burning.

Over Sussex and Kent
The Wittershams stand -
Though many's the home
Lies blasted and bent;
Though many a site
On Down and on Weald
From town to the sea
Will be rubble this night
If you ken the grim Fox with his coat so black
And his firey brush cocked over his back,
You will ken the heart beat with the run of that pack
And the lift of the heart at returning

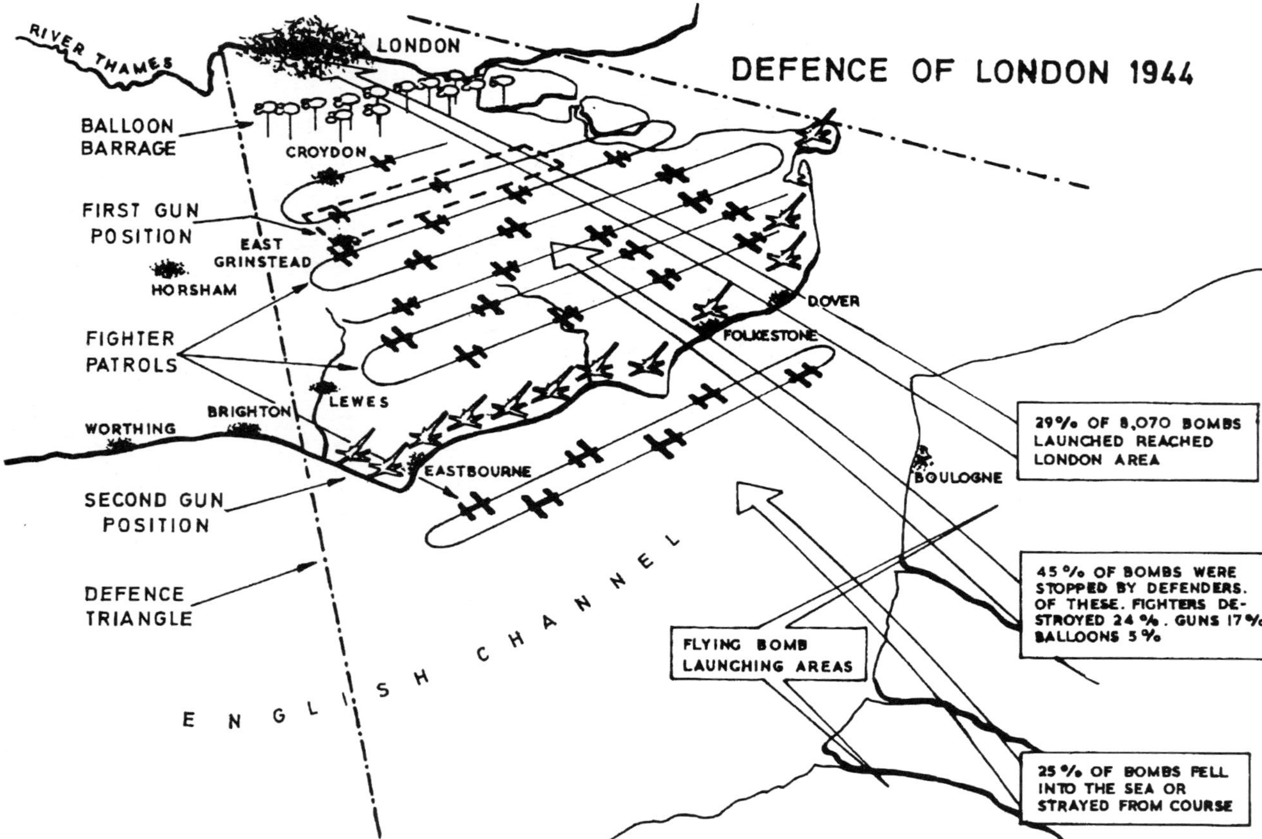
DEFENCE OF LONDON 1944
RIVER THAMES
LONDON
BALLOON BARRAGE
CROYDON
FIRST GUN POSITION
EAST GRINSTEAD
HORSHAM
FIGHTER PATROLS
LEWES
BRIGHTON
WORTHING
EASTBOURNE
SECOND GUN POSITION
DEFENCE TRIANGLE
ENGLISH CHANNEL
DOVER
FOLKESTONE
BOULOGNE
29% OF 8,070 BOMBS LAUNCHED REACHED LONDON AREA
45% OF BOMBS WERE STOPPED BY DEFENDERS. OF THESE. FIGHTERS DESTROYED 24%. GUNS 17% BALLOONS 5%
FLYING BOMB LAUNCHING AREAS
25% OF BOMBS FELL INTO THE SEA OR STRAYED FROM COURSE

ASHFORD and RURAL C.D. AREA

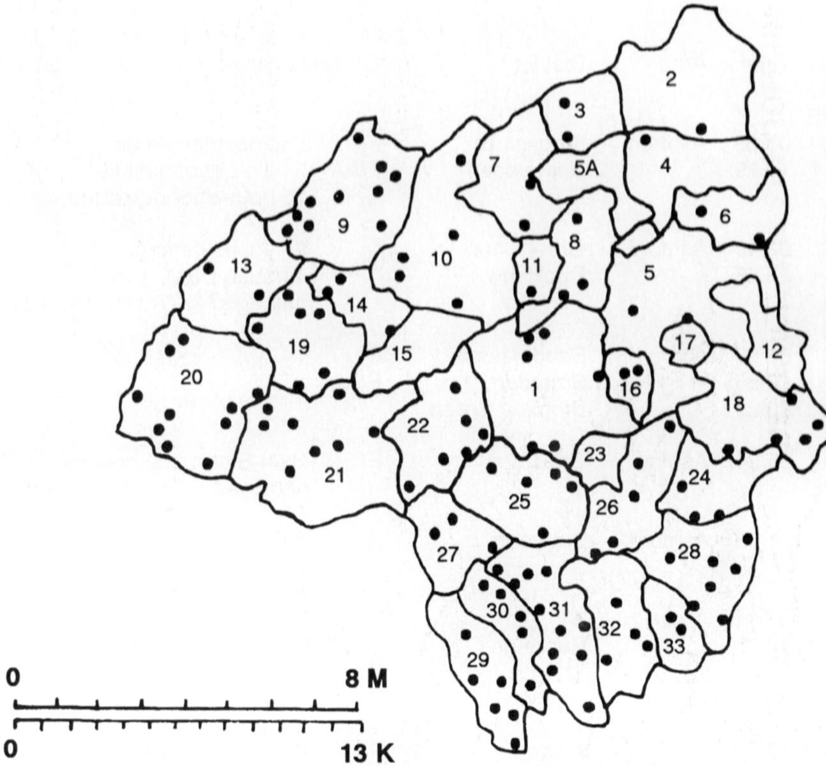

1 ASHFORD URBAN
2 CHILHAM
3 MOLASH
4 GODMERSHAM
5 WYE
5A WYE (DETACHED)
6 CRUNDALE
7 CHALLOCK
8 BOUGHTON ALUPH
9 CHARING
10 WESTWELL
11 EASTWELL
12 HASTINGLEIGH
13 EGERTON
14 LITTLE CHART
15 HOTHFIELD
16 HINXHILL
17 BROOK
18 BRABOURNE
19 PLUCKLEY
20 SMARDEN
21 BETHERSDEN
22 GREAT CHART
23 SEVINGTON
24 SMEETH
25 KINGSNORTH
26 MERSHAM
27 SHADOXHURST
28 ALDINGTON
29 WAREHORN
30 ORLESTONE
31 RUCKINGE
32 BILSINGTON
33 BONNINGTON

ASHFORD BOROUGH, URBAN and RURAL C.D. DISTRICTS

Key:- AA = Ack-ack F = Fighter attack

Date	Time	Area	District	Cause	Location/Incident/Damage
JUNE					
16.6	01.05	Ashford	Kingsnorth		Exploded in the air
	10.29		Bethersden	F/AA	3 miles W of airfield 15 houses Sl damaged
17.6	03.45	Ashford	Great Chart		6 houses damaged
	23.45		Ruckinge		1 house DEM, 1 Badly damaged 1K. 1 Ser. Inj. 3 Sl. Inj
18.6	06.56	Ashford	Shadoxhurst	F	
	16.55		Smarden	F/AA	
	20.25		Bromley Green		
22.6	05.24	Ashford	Orlestone	F	Ham Street 100 houses damaged 1 Ser. Inj, 12 Sl.Inj.
23.6	21.03	Ashford	Smarden	F	Superficial damage to houses in village - widespread Buckles Bakers and 2 other shops DEM 2 Sl. Inj.
	23.33		Ruckinge		Lone Barn Meadow
24.6	06.18	Ashford	Charing	F	Newlands Camp, military casualties 47 K. 28 Ser. Inj
	06.22		Smarden	F	Bartley Poultry Farm 5 K. 1 Ser. Inj.
25.6	23.26	Ashford	Pluckley	F	
26.6	03.48	Ashford	Bethersden	F	
	14.22		Willesborough	F	
27.6	17.35	Ashford	Hothfield	AA	Near Church-damage 2 Sl. Inj.
29.6	11.25	Ashford	Orlestone	F	Bromley Green 4 bungalows slightly damaged 2 Ser.Inj, 1 Sl. Inj.
	12.31		Great Chart	F	
	13.15		Shadoxhurst	F	
	22.16		Aldington	F	2 Sl. Inj.

30.6	10.17	Ashford	Kingsnorth	F	
	20.18		Molash	F	Howletts Farm - Farm buildings and cottage DEM. 1 Sl. Inj.
	22.21		Egerton	F	Elvey Farm
JULY					
03.7	04.51	Ashford	Kingsnorth		Bilham? Farm
	18.28		Charing	F	
05.7	16.45	Ashford	Challock	F	Eastwell Park
	17.45		Charing	F	2 Sl Inj.
	17.46		Pluckley	AA	6 houses major Dam. 12 ser. dam. 240 Sl. dam. 9 Sl Inj.
	18.16		Orlestone	F	
	21.15		Crundale	F	
07.7	00.08	Ashford	Orlestone	F	
	12.54		Pluckley	F	Rushbrooke Farm 2 Sl In
	13.37			F	Newhouse Farm
	15.17			F	
	16.50		Orlestone	F	
	17.07		Ruckinge	F	Houses wrecked 1K 2 Ser Inj
	17.36			F	1 Sl Inj.
	21.24		Bethersden	F	30 houses slight damaged
	23.36		Warehorne	F	40 Acre Farm
08.7	04.32	Ashford	Ruckinge	F	
	21.29		Great Chart	F	
	21.37		Orlestone	F	Capel Road
	21.47		Bilsington	F	
	23.10		Bethersden	F	
	23.15		Hothfield	F	
10.7	15.05	Ashford	Charing	F	Charing Heath
	22.32		Ruckinge	F	
11.7	17.40	Ashford	Bonnington		
	19.32		Hothfield	AA	
	19.32		Smeeth		On Railway line
	19.43		Charing Heath		
	20.50		Bethersden	F	Nr Etchden Farm 1 Sl. Inj.
13.7	16.21	Ashford		F	Slight damage to 75 houses 1 Ser. Inj. 2 Sl. Inj.
14.7	15.15	Ashford	Pluckley	F	
	15.15		Wye	F	1 Sl. Inj.
15.7	15.15	Ashford	Bethersden	F	
	17.30	Ashford		F	600 houses slight damage

16.7	00.19	Ashford		AA	
	00.39	Ashford	Sevington	F	
	10.38	Ashford	Kingsnorth	F	Damage to property
17.7	05.12	Ashford	Ruckinge		
18.7	01.12	Ashford	Bethersden	F	2 Ser. Inj. from No 305 LAABaty
	19.39		Westwell	F	
19.7	08.38	Ashford	Aldington	F	Church Lane
	12.10		Bethersden	F	
	13.36		Charing	F	Charing Heath
	17.26		Great Chart	F	
20.7	01.06	Ashford	Bethersden	F	
	03.17		Smarden	F	Burnt House Farm, Swift Green Sev. damage to house & buildings
	07.27	Ashford	Egerton	F	
	07.28		Hothfield	F	
21.7	14.27	Ashford	Westwell	F	1 Sl. Inj.
22.7	02.31	Ashford	Boughton Aluph	AA	Eastwell Park
	13.15		Pluckley	F	Exploded in air
	14.35		Orlestone	F	Ham Street
	17.06		Shadoxhurst	F	Exploded in air
	17.09		Brabourne	F	
	17.26		Mersham	F	
	18.00		Little Chart	F	
	21.23		Smeeth	F	House DEM. 2 Ser. Inj. 1 Sl. Inj.
23.7	08.14	Ashford	Mersham	F	Little Stone Green Farm
	08.25			F	
	08.29		Bonnington	F	At American aerodrome - hanger damaged 2 Sl. Inj. - military
24.7	05.28		Crundale	F	
	15.04		Eastwell		Farmhouse buildings and cottages damaged 1 Sl Inj.
	21.33	Ashford	Wye	F	Coombe Grove Farm
	21.33		Little Chart		
26.7	01.05	Ashford	Charing	F	1 house Ser. Dam. 11 Sl. Dam.
	06.34		Warehorne	F	Slight Damage to Bridge Farm
	06.36		Great Chart	F	New Street Farm & 5 houses Dam.

26.7	14.25		Hinxhill	F	Slight Dam. to Blackwall Farm and Great Bromley Farm
27.7	17.55	Ashford	Hastingleigh	F	
	21.19		Bilsington	F	
	23.58		Shadoxhurst	F	
28.7	13.22	Ashford	Smarden	F	5 houses Ser. Dam. 12 Sl. Dam. 1 Ser. Inj. 2 Sl. Inj.
	13.27		Brabourne		2 bungalows DEM, 10houses Ser. Dam. 1 K. 3 Ser. Inj. 1 Sl. Inj.
	22.50		Hastingleigh	AA	
29.7	14.18	Ashford	Hastingleigh		South Hill Farm damaged
	21.50		Hastingleigh	F	Court Lodge Farm
	22.50		Aldington	AA	
30.7	13.50	Ashford	Smarden		Damage to houses and Malt House Farmhouse 2 Ser. Inj. 4 Sl. Inj.
	13.55		Bilsington	AA	
	16.04		Bilsington	AA	Pear Tree Farm
	23.46		Challock	F	Clock House Farm 3 Sl. Inj.
31.7	07.21	Ashford	Shadoxhurst	F	Blind Green Farm
	08.45		Brabourne	F	
	08.56		Charing	F	
	15.15		Charing	F	Little Hook Farm
	17.26	Ashford		F	2 Sl. Inj.
	17.31		Pluckley	F	20 houses Dam. 2 Ser. Inj.
	21.10		Warehorne	F	
AUGUST					
03.8	02.14	Ashford	Aldington	AA	
	02.17		Bilsington	AA	Same incident as above?
	04.14		Mersham	AA	
	04.30		Smarden	AA	Damage to Romden Castle
	08.19		Smarden	F	Damage to 1 house
	09.20		Warehorne	F	
	10.16		Westwell	F	
	10.19		Great Chart		New Street Farm
04.8	02.00	Ashford	Charing	F	Brockton Farm
	02.41		Ruckinge		
	15.44		Challock	F	Eastwell Park
	16.30		Chilham	F	Chilham Park
	18.56		Aldington	F	Goldwell Farm house damaged

04.8	19.03	Ashford		F	Catholic School, Victoria Park 3 ser Inj. Flour Mills, Co-Op Bakery, Laundry all dam 21 Sl Inj.
05.8	19.04	Ashford	Challock	F	
06.8	05.35	Ashford	Aldington	AA	
	13.31		Ruckinge	F	
	17.03		Great Chart	F	On airfield, minor damage to Possingham Farm, superficial damage to Washington Farm.
07.8	06.04	Ashford	Smeeth	F	Damage to farmhouse & cottages
	07.20		Orlestone	F	
	11.03		Bonnington	F	
10.8	21.02	Ashford	Great Chart	F	Brideswell? Farm
	21.04		Bethersden	F	Same incident as above?
	21.05		Ruckinge		
	21.20		Hinxhill		
11.8	14.05	Ashford	Brabourne	AA	
	14.07		Kingsnorth	F	
	14.16		Brabourne	F	
	14.32		Aldington		
12.8	01.38	Ashford	Orlestone	AA	
13.8	06.20	Ashford	Orlestone	AA	Some damage
	08.00		Aldington	AA	(C.C Type) Marwood Farm
15.8	09.30	Ashford	Hothfield	F	Exploded in air 2 Sl. Inj.
	04.30		Hothfield		Exploded in air
	14.23		Ruckinge		
	14.25		Boughton Aluph	F	
	15.39		Godmersham	F	
16.8	05.21	Ashford	Boughton Aluph		2 houses damaged
	16.42		Hothfild	F	4 cottages slightly damaged
	17.31		Orlestone		
	18.34	Ashford		F	Between Railway Works and Railway Station 4 Ser. Inj. 5 Sl. Inj.
	19.09		Westwell	F	
	19.10		Brabourne	AA	
	19.45		Aldington	AA	
	20.04		Little Chart	F	Damage to Church & Chart Court Farm house
	20.30		Charing	F	

17.8	07.40	Ashford	Wye	F	Damage to 2 houses and farm buildings
	09.13		Hinxhill	F	Goodcheap Farm
	20.28		Ruckinge	F	2 hses bad Dam. 1 Ser Inj
19.8	14.30	Ashford	Aldington		Damage to 3 houses 1 Ser. Inj. 1 Sl . Inj.
20.8	11.45	Ashford	Pluckley	AA	1 house Sl. Dam 1 Sl. Inj.
	12.15		Challock		Church' & 2 cottages damaged
21.8	04.07	Ashford	Westwell		Hothfield Halt, damage to 7 houses
	12.33		Bonnington	AA	Damage to farm
23.8	09.07	Ashford	Pluckley	F	Damage to 10 houses & barn Dowle Street Farm
	09.08		Godmersham		Pope Street Farm
	09.20		Great Chart	F	Exploded in air, superficial dam to 9 buildings
	20.48		Bethersden	F	Damage to Dynes Farmhouse and buildings.
24.8	02.50	Ashford	Kingsnorth	AA	20 houses and shops damaged
	07.43		Molash		In air - Dryland Farm house
	17.46		Aldington		Sev. Dam. to 200 houses 1 Ser. Inj.
	18.20		Smarden		
	21.12		Warehorne	AA	
27.8	07.48	Ashford	Ruckinge	F	
28.8	14.43	Ashford	Chilham	F	Slight damage to Stile Farm house
29.8	17.31	Ashford	Smarden		Road to Bethersden blocked
30.8	09.36	Ashford	Boughton Aluph	F	
	07.38		Wye		
31.8	09.12	Ashford	Aldington	AA	Contained leaflets

PROPAGANDA V-1's

Some of the V-1's also contained propaganda leaflets which were designed to be distributed when the missile exploded.

Colonel Jack ROBINSON ARLINGTON, Texas U.S.A.	*416th Fighter-Bomber Group based at ALG 417 Chilmington Great Chart, Nr Ashford*	Reactions to the first V-1 incident, etc

Early on the morning of 13th June the V-1 flying bomb attack started, and Ashford was in a direct line between the launching sites and London, in the midst of the ack-ack gun belt set up to defend the city. On the night of the 15th June, Ashford saw its first V-1, and the guns opened up like a chapter from 'Buck Rogers' lacing the sky with tracer bullets. To add to the confusion, a telephone call from H.Q. had warned of parachute landings on the coast taking place at the same time so our unrehearsed Group Defence Plan went into operation. All personnel were floundering around in the dark, in all sorts of night dress and webbing equipment, but with the essential steel helmets, as shrapnel from ack-ack guns was falling all round. Some dug fox holes and slept in them, and all kept their ears cocked for the ominous sound of motor cut-outs.

On another occasion the 514th Fighter Squadron was lined up on the north end of the runway ready for take off, when the leader saw a V-1 coming directly at him, or so he thought. Fortunately it just missed and came down just across the road at the north end of the runway. We had people injured from Allied ground and aircraft guns much flak fell around us, but I do not remember anyone being seriously injured. One of our pilots had a .50 ins calibre machine gun bullet go through his leg above the knee, but he was lucky as it divided everything and did not cause real extended damage. He soon returned to flying, but was later killed in action.

Mrs D. SHOOBRIDGE CHARING, Kent.	*Civilian - living at 'Marness', Ruckinge.*	Injured when home was hit by a V-1.

During the last war I lived at 'Marness' Ruckinge, a large solidly built bungalow, which stood alone in fields and had been turned into a small holding with various animals, etc. On Friday 7th July 1944, my sister, who was 15 1/2 years old, my brother who was seven years old, and I just approaching my 16th birthday were just sitting down to have our tea, when we heard a doodlebug coming. We heard a Spitfire go up after it, then the machine gun fire. The doodlebug's engine stopped so we ducked for cover under the table, but it was too late. We had a direct hit as the doodlebug landed right in the middle of the bungalow. The blast killed my little brother, knocked out my sister and blew me through a two-foot thick wall and I ended up, suspended by my legs, under the bath.

I waited and listened, then I heard a man's voice so I shouted for help. As soon as he heard me, he called for silence, then asked me to direct him to us. By this time there were dozens of people there trying to get us out. Suddenly we all heard another doodlebug, then the Spitfire's guns - again the engine stopped. The man called for everyone to take cover as this second doodlebug was heading straight for us, but the pilot of the Spitfire kept firing his guns. Luckily for us he shot one wing off the doodlebug thus tipping it over; it landed on the farm buildings of the next farm, killing the farmer's prize bull, but nobody was hurt as they were all helping rescue us. My brother was killed, my sister had shock and bruises and I had badly crushed legs and bruises. I was buried for two hours before I was finally got out, feeling very dirty, and embarrassed, because the blast had torn all my clothes to shreds.

Mr R.R.MAY ASHFORD, Kent.	*Apprentice - Southern Railway Works, Ashford.*	Incidents at Ashford station & S.R. works.

I was working at the Kimberly works and as it was one of the main Southern Railway workshops, we had Air Raid Spotters and warnings were given about planes and V-1's etc. We were told to go to the shelters whenever the warning was given, but as us lads wanted to see all the action going on outside, we would go to the Bofors gun that the work's Home Guard were operating and we saw it firing at a V-1. It was going low over the Torrington Road area the sky was peppered with black dots and going through all this was a V-1. Then to our horror, and to the gun crew's, we saw a flight of about eight U.S. P-47 Thunderbolt fighters. I think that they were returning from a mission in Northern France and were coming in to land at their airfield at Kingsnorth. Anyway, these planes had to take violent evasive action, and a sort of Red Arrows display followed. They managed to avoid being shot down but unfortunately the V-1 escaped in the melee and headed on in the direction of Maidstone and disappeared from our sight.

I was then moved to the erecting shop in the main works, to start my apprenticeship; my next close encounter being on 16th August 1944. There were a lot of workers at the rail works who came from Folkestone Dover, Deal and Canterbury so the evening trains were always full. On that evening

I was standing in the train corridor, on the side facing the railway works, when I saw a V-1, coming in quite low, in line with the main railway line. It was about over Willesborough, and we all thought that it was going to pass over, but as it got closer an R.A.F. Meteor suddenly came out of the sky and slowed down in front of the V-1. It seemed to nudge the V-1's short wing tip which caused the V-1 to go haywire, it coughed and spluttered then silence - then it just dropped like a stone; but the jet just carried on its way over the Great Chart area. There was a loud bang, an explosion, and it rained boxes as the V-1 had hit the goods storage area by the station. The signal man in his box had a lucky escape and a few steam engines were damaged, but a V-1 didn't reach London. Empty ammunition boxes and other debris were soon cleared up and our train left for home - a little late!

Mr D.W.A JOHNSON ASHFORD, Kent.	*Schoolboy - The North Central School, Ashford.*	Incidents at Newtown and in school garden.

I was 13 years old at the time, and lived in the railway houses in Newtown Road. On one occasion my friend and I were in a field across the Canterbury Road, at Willesborough when we saw a V-1, approximately 400 feet up, with seven fighters (a Tempest, a Spitfire, a Meteor and others) all firing at it and all the colours of the rainbow were coming out of this doodlebug's jet. I said to my friend, "If that blows up, the blast could kill us!" It dived down onto the Newtown Road area, and we ran home like hares, fearing our houses had been hit, but it had hit the signal box just outside Ashford Railway station.

I attended the Ashford North Central School near Essella Road. One day we were working in the school garden, when a doodlebug approached above the low clouds. I heard a spluttering sound, then deadly silence. I fell into a deep trench on the edge of the garden to avoid the blast. About twenty of the boys and the Master ran into a garden shed, but I thought that they should be lying flat on the ground! This time the doodlebug flew on much further than expected before it fell to earth and exploded the one ton of TNT in its nose.

My wife lived in Godinton Road, behind the Stanhay Workshop, where I believe ammunition was prepared. A doodlebug scored a direct hit on the works. Her father had just got inside the house when a large piece of shrapnel fell into their yard, while another piece was found right on their back doorstep, their door was blown off its hinges, and their ceilings crashed down with the blast.

Mr P. TOWNSEND RAMSGATE, Kent.	*Radar Technician on SCR 584 sets, and home visits.*	Kippings Cross, Near Tonbridge; Willesborough Lees near Ashford.

In June 1944 I was at a school of instruction near Leicester where the new equipment was the latest American heavy AA radar set, known as SCR 584. No sooner had the course started than the V-1 offensive commenced. Soon I began to receive disturbing letters from my wife, who at the time was carrying our first child. She lived at Willesborough Lees, on the outskirts of Ashford, and in front of her cottage was a grass field with a prominent crater on the far side caused by an aeroplane from Wye aerodrome crashing there during WW1. Now this spot was occupied by a searchlight and its crew, and she went on to describe how she, and her neighbours, were spending most of the days and nights in their air raid shelters as the searchlight party blazed away at the on-coming flying bombs with their Lewis machine gun.

I was anxious to visit my wife and see if there was anything I could suggest to improve her way of life, also I hoped to see a V-1. By an annoying coincidence my visit occurred during a break in the steady flow of the bombs, the last one had gone over some ten minutes before I arrived; the next arrived some twenty minutes after I had departed! Back at my regular base in Plymouth I waited to find out what the future held and was impatient to move on to somewhere more active. In the event, it came as something of a surprise when I was posted to Kippings Cross, near Tonbridge Kent. Here I discovered that SCR584 Radar was one of the main keys to the success in the fight against the V-1s.

Despite the fact that I now knew that I was doing something really vital, there was always one cloud on my horizon. I soon knew where the main corridors of approach of the V-1s were, and so I was aware that many of them passed over Ashford, also many were shot down by the R.A.F. *en route*, which sometimes resulted in people on the ground being tragically killed. So when on one of my days off, I visited my wife, she immediately dragged me out into one of Farmer Brett's fields to view the result of 'their' bomb. The searchlight site had now been equipped with a Bofors gun, which had done nothing to calm the nerves of the locals. Whenever a target was engaged it always started at low angle over the roofs of the houses, and as I knew, a disabled bomb could come down on the site or very close.

The V-1 had been shot down and had crashed in soft earth, and I was surprised at the size of the hole. Huge lumps of earth, some the size of a small room, had been lifted bodily and flung many yards. It wasn't possible to tell how deep it was, as at a depth of about twelve feet it was filled with water. An attempt had been made to fill it using a small farm tractor fitted with a bulldozer attachment, but the driver had lost control, with the result that the vehicle was half-way down the side of the crater, perched precariously on it's 'dozer' bit, and would need a crane to retrieve it. It looked quite puny in its fly on the wall situation, and brought home an idea of the tremendous force of the explosion. As my wife chattered gaily on about how this force had brought down a cloud of dust, earwigs and spiders from the roof of their shelter, I looked glumly across to her house and thought, 'a couple of hundred yards to the left and I could have been a widower'.

The Allied advance began to overrun the V-1 launching sites and as soon as this happened, the SCR 584 sets had to be returned to the U.S. Forces, as they urgently needed them for their own use. Then came the day when the victorious Allies captured the sites launching the bombs that came in over Hastings, passing over Tonbridge area on their way to London. However, they were still coming over the Folkestone area. My wife had now presented me with a beautiful daughter, and she told me how, during her confinement, she had laid in bed watching the doodle bugs approaching and passing overhead.

Mrs J.M.HARRISON Shooters Hill LONDON	*Schoolgirl at Ashford & Gravesend in 1944*	Near miss incident at Godinton Park, Ashford

In 1944 I was living at Ashford with my parents. From our house in Sackville Crescent we had an uninterrupted view across the fields on either side of the main railway line from London and Ashford. I well remember one occasion when I was sharing my bedroom with a friend who was staying with us at the time and we were lying in bed, listening to the sound of a flying bomb approaching. Suddenly there was nothing but silence; silence spelling danger. We both jumped out of bed, ran down the stairs, passing my father rushing up to fetch my baby sister, and joined my mother in the cupboard under the stairs. My father was halfway down the stairs again carrying the baby, when we heard a dull thud We emerged from our refuge to find the dining room floor covered with red currents, which my mother had been 'topping and tailing' into a bowl on her lap. She had dropped it when she and my father had seen the doodlebug above the trees, apparently heading straight for our corner of the Crescent.

The following morning we found out, from the milkman, the story behind our lucky escape. A nearby anti-aircraft battery had managed to divert that V-1 away from our house and into Godinton Park. However, during a short stay in Gravesend, we found things were not quite the same there. The fighters only pursued the flying bombs as far as the second line of defence, this being the barrage balloons at Wrotham. When a V-1 hit a balloon cable the shock was usually sufficient to stop its engine, but often it glided in silence for some miles before crashing to earth, so there was no warning of its imminent arrival. I was terrified throughout our visit and was glad to return to the more familiar conditions in the Ashford area.

Mrs Patricia LA TROBE, HYTHE, Kent.	*In Women's Land Army at Coombe Farm, Brabourne.*	Incidents seen from farms on North Downs.

The first V-1 I saw was at Penstock Hall on the North Downs as we could see from Dungeness to Folkestone, even further on a clear day. The first one we heard was at evening time; we heard a peculiar noise which was unlike any other plane that had ever come over. We went out and there was this thing with a flame behind it, it went right over our house and we all stood in the open 'gaping' at it. We didn't know what it was; we had had no warning that these things were coming, and I don't think we did hear until a day or two after; we just wondered what this peculiar thing was. It was quite a long time afterwards, when they started coming over more and more regularly, that we got used to the noise; it was an uneven sound, with a cracking to it.

One time I saw about fourteen brought down in five minutes, as far as I remember, it was the first time the fighters (Tempests) were able to catch up with the V-1s in level flight. There were the coastal guns going, bringing down a few, and we could see the puffs of smoke, and at the same time, the ones that got through the ack-ack barrage were being attacked by the planes right over where we were; there were just great explosions and puffs of smoke going up, like nothing on earth, just below us on the Downs. A few still got through and they had to contend with the barrage balloons.

The one that landed nearest to us was in a field behind the pub at Brabourne. I was with some other Landgirls and a tractor driver when the engine switched off and it started coming down. It had turned and was coming absolutely straight for our field. We grabbed each other and leapt into a ditch then, for no apparent reason, it turned completely round again, and landed about two fields away. A woman who had stinted her family of sugar for ages to make jam and to bottle fruit, had jars standing on a table in her back bedroom. The explosion burst all the jars and their contents cascaded down the staircase. It also took all the windows out of the cottages, and blew some tiles off the roofs, but it didn't injure anybody.

Major General Cameron addressing some American anti-aircraft gunners at St Mary's Bay near New Romney. Their SCR854 Radar with sand-bagged cabin and aerial dish (on left) guided anti-aircraft guns onto their targets. (photo via S.E.Newspapers No 29A/702/16/83)

After the main V-1 campaign had ended, air launched flying bombs still caused damage and casualties.
Above: Clearing up taking place in Carrington Road Dartford after one such incident on 8th November 1944.
(Photo Dartford Library via C.R Munday)

DARTFORD and MEDWAY C.D. AREA

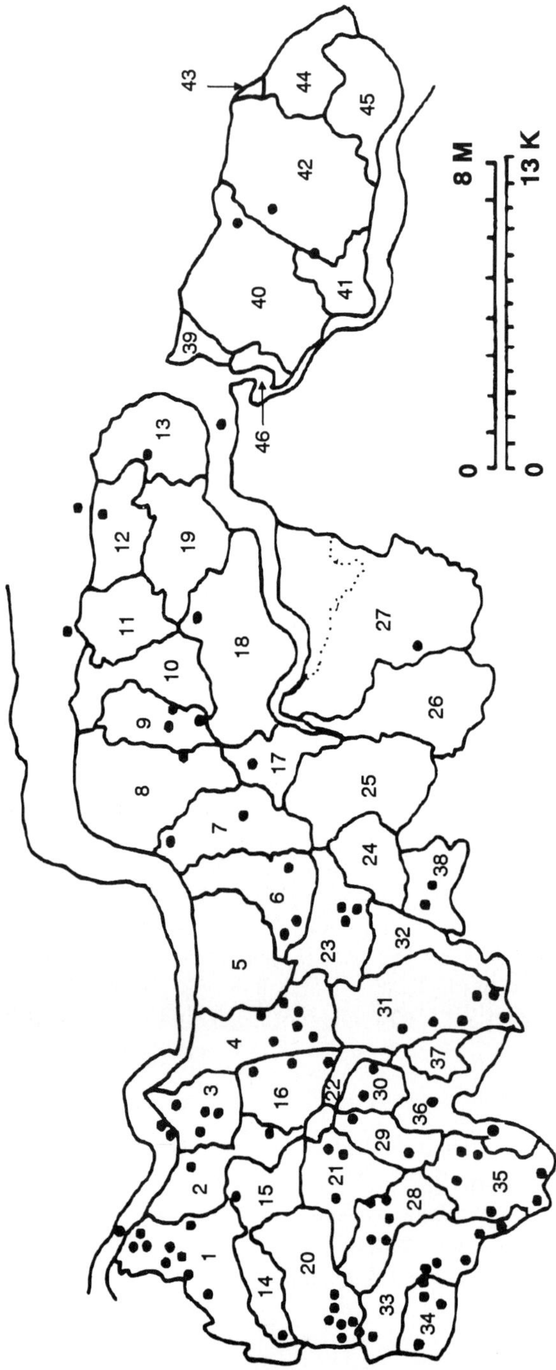

DARTFORD and MEDWAY C.D. AREA

1	DARTFORD BOROUGH	2	STONE	3	SWANCOMBE
4	NORTHFLEET	5	BOROUGH OF GRAVESEND	6	SHORNE
7	HIGHAM	8	CLIFFE	9	COOLING
10	HIGH HALSTOW	11	ST. MARY, HOO	12	ALL HALLOWS
13	ISLE OF GRAIN	14	WILMINGTON	15	DARENTH
16	SOUTHFLEET	17	FRINDSBURY EXTRA	18	HOO ST. WERBURGH
19	STOKE	20	SUTTON AT HONE	21	HORTON KIRBY
22	LONGFIELD	23	COBHAM	24	CUXTON
25	BOROUGH OF ROCHESTER	26	BOROUGH OF CHATHAM	27	BOROUGH OF GILLINGHAM
28	FARNINGHAM	29	FALKHAM	30	HARTLEY
31	MEOPHAM	32	LUDDLESDOWN	33	EYNSFORD
34	LULLINGSTONE	35	WEST KINGSDOWN	36	ASH
37	RIDLEY	38	HALLING	39	SHEERNESS U.D.
40	MINSTER-IN-SHRPPY	41	ELMLEY	42	EASTCHURCH
43	WARDEN	44	LEYSDOWN	45	HARTY
46	BOROUGH OF QUEENSBOROUGH				

DARTFORD BOROUGH and RURAL, GRAVESEND BOROUGH, ISLE of SHEPPEY, MEDWAY GROUP, NORTHFLEET, and STROOD RURAL C.D DISTRICTS

Key AA = ack-ack fire BB = Barrage Balloon; F = Fighter attack

Date	Time	Area	District	Cause	Location/Incident/Damage
JUNE					
13.6	04.20	Dartford R	Swanscombe		Bean - Caused blast damage
16.6	02.00	Medway	Chatham		2 Ser. Inj. by shrapnel
	03.53	Dartford B			Shepherds Lane/Princes Rd 8 houses DEM. 6 Sev dam. 1 K. 6 Sl.Inj.
	03.40	Dartford R	Stone		Stones Wood, Bean 2 Sl. Inj.
			Eynsford		Crockenhill 1 Sl. Inj.
			Lullingstone		2 miles W. of Eynsford Station
	05.20	Medway	Queenborough		Fell in creek
17.6	23.59	Strood R	Hoo		
18.6	03.05	Dartford B			80 houses damaged
	03.40	Dartford R	Sutton-at-Hone		Swanley Junct. on school grounds St. Mary's Road 3 Sl. Inj.
	11.46		Wilmington	F	6 Ser. Inj.
	11.55	Strood R	Meopham		3 houses Dam. 1 Sl. Inj.
	20.35		Lullingstone	F/AA	Damage to Castle
20.6	18.32	Dartford R	Sutton-at-Hone	F	Rear of Highland Cottage, Highland Hill 30 houses Dam. 4 Ser Inj. 12 Sl Inj
22.6	03.04	Dartford R	Horton Kirby	BB	Hit cable and exploded in cornfield rear of New Barn Rd.
	18.45		Southfleet		Potato field Brentfield Road
	18.45		Lullingstone	F	
	19.02		Horton Kirby		Rear of Horton Kirby School
23.6	01.56	Dartford R	Kingsdown	BB	Damage to R.A.F Camp
	08.10	Dartford B			80 houses damaged, 5 Sl. Inj.
	15.05				Fell in river
	17.33	Dartford R	Falkham	BB	Crashed Brands Hatch Rd, Falkham 2 houses Dam. 3 Sl. Inj.

25.6	04.28	Medway	Rochester	F/AA	No144 Brompton Farm Road, 2 houses Ser. Dam. 24 Minor Dam. 130 Sl. Dam 2 Ser. Inj. 4 Sl. Inj.
26.6	00.45	Dartford R	Kingsdown		
	04.40		Ash	BB	
27.6	03.05	Dartford R	Horton Kirby		Nr Viaduct S. Darenth 3 Sl. Inj.
	05.46		Eynsford		100 yds E of Wested Farm 3 Sl. Inj.
	20.32	Medway	Gillingham	F	Darland
	22.33	Dartford R	Farningham		
28.6	08.41	Strood R			S.W of Gravesend airfield
	13.43	Strood R	Meopham	F	
	21.30	Dartford R	Hartley	F	
	22.04		Southfleet	BB	New Barn 1 Sl. Inj.
JULY					
01.7	02.55	Dartford B		AA	Joydens Wood
	07.05	Strood R	Cliffe		24 houses Serious Dam. 30/40 Sl. Dam. 3 Ser. Inj. 7 Sl. Inj.
	07.40	Dartford R	Farningham	BB	Nr A20 property damaged 11 Sl. Inj.
	09.08	Dartford B			Marshes nr KA13 Factory, considerable damage
	10.28	Dartford R	Lullingstone	BB	3 Ser. Inj. 1 Sl. Inj.
	10.49	Strood R	Cooling		2 houses damaged
	11.37		Higham		16 houses Serious damage 4 Ser.Inj. 12. Sl. Inj.
	12.25	Dartford R	Sutton-at-Hone		
	12.45		Eynsford	BB	W. of Austin Lodge Lane
	14.30	Dartford R	Kingsdown		400 yds W of Ashen Grove Road East Hill
	23.30		Sutton-at-Hone	BB	Ramswood - 34 houses Dam. 1 Ser. Inj.
02.7	04.40	Dartford R	Horton Kirby		
03.7	12.18	Dartford R	Falkham	AA	
05.7	01.45	Dartford R	Northfleet		
	17.40	Gravesend	Chalk	F	150 houses Dam. 1 Ser. Inj. 2 Sl. Inj.
	18.20	Dartford R	Ash cum Ridley	AA	
		Strood R	Meopham	BB	

08.7	03.20	Medway	Sheppey	F	
09.7	14.32	Dartford	Horton Kirby	BB	
	21.25		Wilmington	F	6 Sl. Inj.
09.7	22.16	Strood R	Shorne	F	Walmer Ave, 1 house DEM. 3 Ser. Dam. 50 Sl. Dam. 1 K. 1 Ser. Inj. 9 Sl. Inj.
10.7	09.11	Dartford R	Eynsford	BB	2 Sl. Inj.
11.7	19.34	Dartford R	Stone		W. of Littlebrook Power Station
15.7	17.29	Dartford R	Kingsdown	BB	
16.7	10.20	Medway	Chatham		Damage to Walderslade from Malling incident (Blue Bell Hill)
17.7	08.20	Dartford R	Darenth	BB	
18.7	02.24	Medway	Sheppey	F	Elmley Park
19.7	02.56	Dartford R	Southfleet	BB	
	03.35		Darenth	BB	
	13.45		Swanscombe	BB	
	19.48	Strood R	Cobham	BB	
21.7	10.18	Dartford R	Lullingstone	BB	
22.7	02.15	Dartford R	Eynsford		Nr Hulbury Farm
	06.25	Strood R	Cooling		in Marshes
	16.38	Dartford R	Eynsford	BB	Nr Austin Lodge
24.7	00.20	Strood R	Cobham	BB	Ashen Bank Wood, 1 R.A.F Sl. Inj
25.7	02.53	Dartford R	Swanscombe	BB	in plantation at Alkerden Farm
26.7	01.20	Dartford R	Kingsdown	BB	Slight damage to property
	04.13		Eynsford	BB	Slight damage to property
	07.49		Farningham		Damage to property 2 Ser Inj. 4 Sl. Inj
	07.55	Strood R	Meopham	BB	Exploded in air
27.7	16.55	Dartford R	Swanscombe		
28.7	13.36	Dartford R	Lullingstone	BB	
29.7	00.18	Dartford R	Northfleet	BB	
	16.00		Stone		Exploded in air
	23.17		Stone		In River, some damage 3 Ser. Inj.

30.7	13.42	Medway	Rochester		Sl. Dam. to 2 cottages 1 Sl. Inj
	13.43	Strood		AA	In Medway
30.7	23.47	Dartford R	Northfleet		Landed on row of houses in Taunton Rd, 80 houses DEM 26 Ser. Dam. 200 Minor Dam. 13 K. 22 Ser. Inj. 69 Sl. Inj.
31.7	15.30	Dartford R	Stone		In river
AUGUST					
02.8	04.10	Dartford R	Farningham		
	06.25		Swanscombe	BB	In a field
03.8	01.20	Dartford B			On Orchard hospital causing fire
	01.25	Dartford R	Southfleet		S.E of station
	01.45		Farningham		Rear of Oliver Crescent 11 Sl. Inj.
	01.55		Northfleet	BB	Miskins Farm
	02.59		Sutton-at-Hone		In field
	03.50	Strood R	Shorne		On Nissen huts in Military area. 6 Military K.
	03.55	Dartford R	Fawkham	BB	2 Sl. Inj.
	04.18	Strood R	Halling		Court Lodge Farm damaged
	08.00	Dartford R	Eynsford	BB	Green Court Road, Crockenhill. 1 Ser. Inj. 4 Sl. Inj.
04.8	03.10	Strood R	All Hallows		In sea off
	03.32	Medway	Gillingham		Hap Wood, Meresborough
	18.10	Dartford R	Ash	BB	
	20.15		Ridley	BB	
	20.30	Medway	Strood		
05.8	16.32	Dartford R	Swanscombe	BB	In river Nr Greenhithe
06.8	17.10	Dartford B			Carrington Rd. 8 houses DEM, 10 Ser Dam 25 Minor Dam. 700 Sl. Dam.10 K. 12 Ser. Inj 95 Sl. Inj.
07.8	07.25	Dartford R	Ridley		Berrys Maple damage to SearchlightStation 1 Ser. Inj.
	07.30		Darenth	F	Gills Farm 1 Sl. Inj
	08.20	Strood R	Cooling		In the marshes
	11.00	Dartford R	Swanscombe		Considerable damage to 4 streets. 20 houses DEM. 300 damaged.2 K. 18 Ser. Inj. 29 Sl. Inj.

08.8	08.50	Strood R	Cuxton	BB	Damage to property
	23.20	Dartford R	Darenth	BB	
10.8	04.20	Strood R	Cobham	BB	(C.C Type) in air
	04.25	Dartford R	Sutton-at-Hone	BB	(C.C Type) slight damage 2 Sl. Inj.
11.8	14.12	Dartford R	Horton Kirby	BB	(C.C type)
12.8	01.34	Dartford R	Horton Kirby	BB	Nr School Lane
	01.48	Gravesend		BB	In field 200 yds N. of Watling St.
	06.15	Dartford R	Longfield	BB	Exploded in air
	06.20	Strood R	Cobham	BB	Exploded in air over Watling St and Malling Cross. 16 houses Damaged.
	23.05	Dartford R	Farningham		Calfstock Lane
14.8	02.14	Dartford R	Ash		Damage to houses
	04.32	Medway	Rochester		(C.C Type) 40 houses slight damage 3 Sl. Inj. Nr Frindsbury Extra
	07.02	Dartford R	Fawkham	BB	Fawkham Green damage to 36 premises1 Ser. Inj. 3 Sl. Inj.
	09.02		Kingsdown		Church Wood, Fawkham Road 1 Sl. Inj.
	15.50	Dartford B		BB	In open field
	19.03	Dartford R	Southfleet		Nr Station 1 Sl. Inj
15.8	17.54	Strood R	Meopham	BB	(C.C Type)
	17.58		Cuxton		Damage to signal box
16.8	07.13	Dartford R	New Ash Green	BB	Chapel Wood
	08.45		Fawkham		In field
	16.45	Medway	Rochester		1 house DEM. 480 Dam 4 K. 1 Ser. Inj.21 Sl. Inj.
	16.48	Strood R	Swanscombe		Damage to Western Cross Farm 5 Sl. Inj
17.8	16.30	Dartford B			Joydens Wood, some damage
19.8	03.15	Dartford B			Littlebrook Farm - slight damage to Joyce Green Hospital
19.8	14.35	Dartford R	Northfleet	BB	(C.C Type) field Nr Broad Dittton Road& Downs Road 40 houses Sl.Dam.
	14.40	Strood R	Hoo		In river
21.8	02.20	Strood R	Meopham	BB	

24.8	19.35	Strood R	Higham		On marsh
28.8	14.15	Dartford R	Stone	F	Exploded in chalk pit - container of propaganda leaflets found in crater. Damage to property & grid near Littlebrook Power Station. 3 Sl. Inj.
	18.30	Sheppey	Eastchurch	F	
30.8	07.49	Dartford R	Darenth	BB	Darenth Training Colony 7 Sl. Inj.
	12.04	Strood R	Halling		(C.C Type)
31.8	08.59	Strood R	Stoke	AA	Isle of Grain minor damage to plant KM3
	11.55		Shorne		

V-1 DEVELOPMENTS

The 'C.C' Type noted above was a development of the V-1 introduced during the later period of the attack using non-strategic materials such as steel.

For those without garden shelters, the brick tunnel kilns of a local cement works provided ideal protection, at Northfleet. These tunnels had been used during the Battle of Britain and the Blitz.
(Photo Kent Messenger via K.C.C)

Mr George DARLING, HYTHE, Kent.	*Worker at Empire Paper Mills, Northfleet.*	Incidents at Swanscombe and Falkham.

It was in the early hours of Tuesday 13th June 1944 that the first flying bombs came over here. I heard, what I thought was a plane, drop a bomb but was curious as I could no longer hear the noise of the aircraft. In fact, I had heard the first flying bomb that dropped in a field at Swanscombe a few miles away. They sounded like heavy bombers, and I 'skidaddled' to the Anderson shelter in the garden even the cats raced for cover as tracer bullets were streaking the sky like Roman Candles.

Generally they did not scare me very much; all the time that their engines kept going, and unless they were making a 'bee-line' in your direction, one was fairly safe. Some dropped like a stone when their engines cut out, but others glided some distance before they landed, and of course, blew up. A few of these caught me unawares and crashed a few hundred yards away. I was working at the Empire Paper Mills at one time, and a flying bomb fell very close, breaking some windows. I was engaged in the crucial task of changing a 'blanket' on one of the paper machines, so I could not dash for cover.

One of the closest that I experienced was while I was staying with my friends a few miles from Northfleet. I heard this dull 'swooshing' sound, it was a doodlebug in a glide. I shouted 'Down everyone!' and flung myself on the ground. The blast made the windows wobble, and a multitudinous series of echoes arose around, possibly deflected from the many barrage balloons nearby. On August 14th I looked out of the air raid shelter and saw a doodlebug suddenly dive onto the village of Falkham Green, wrecking many houses, and four people being hurt. An orange circle of light appeared to expand from the explosion, which I heard in duplicate, the first coming through the earth, and the second through the air, from about a mile away.

In the autumn of 1944 there were some mysterious bangs like exploding bombs, but not heralded by the air-raid siren. I overheard an Air Raid Warden say that he was not supposed to discuss what they were. Then on Saturday, 11th November, news was published officially that they were the V-2 rockets, previously referred to as being 'gas main explosions'. One V-2 crater which I saw near my friend's house in the country was large enough to bury a bus in, it was pear shaped with the pointed end in the direction from where it had come.

Mr Peter H HALES RAMSGATE Kent. — *Schoolboy - living at Park Avenue, Northfleet.* — First Kent V-1 at Swanscombe and the balloon barrage.

In 1944 I was living with my parents in Park Avenue, Northfleet. One particular night in June that summer the air raid siren had sounded, but we did not go to our shelter; my dad and I went into our garden to see the searchlights and the other activities which were happening. Things were fairly quiet for a time then we became aware of an unusual phut, phut, phut sound approaching from the East. We looked up towards where the sound was coming and saw what appeared to be an aircraft with a flaming tail approaching. When this 'aircraft' got just past us the noise stopped, the flame went out, and all went quite for a few seconds then came an explosion; we had seen our first doodlebug.

Another memory I have is of coming home from school one lunchtime (as I couldn't stand school dinners). There was an air raid on at the time and I had just got on my bike outside our front door when I heard a doodlebug approaching. I saw it hit the cable of the barrage balloon which was sited at the top of our road, so I dropped my bike and dived behind our garden wall. I believe that one also fell in the Swanscombe/Crayford area. I then carried on to school - what an excuse for being late back from lunch!

Mr John BROWN SWANLEY, Kent. — *Schoolboy - living in Havelock Road, Dartford.* — Incidents in Dartford and Brook St. Erith.

One incident occurred on Sunday evening 9th July at the junction of Princes Road near Maiden Lane, and as I remember it was a beautiful summers evening; the klaxon sounded at about 8.00pm, but there was not the usual V-1 engine noise. Suddenly a gliding bomb appeared in the SE travelling in our direction at a low altitude; as it neared Princes Rd it began to roll from side to side, one could hear the 'swish' of air rushing past the wings. Finally, it went into a shallow dive and hit the trolley bus wires in Dartford Road, several people waiting at the bus stop were killed, and many houses were damaged.

A very close experience happened on 18th July, at the Brook Street Schools in Erith. I was playing in a boys evening cricket match at the school, when at about 7.00pm, the local warning sounded but we carried on until somebody noticed a gliding bomb some distance off and seemingly moving very slowly, but nevertheless coming in our direction. We all thought that it would probably drop before reaching us but it kept on going until over the field. Most of us were terrified and rooted to the spot, not knowing which way to run; all I recall is being aware of a considerable heat emanating from the bomb. It then did two rolls and dived to the left, fortunately away from us, so we ran in the opposite direction and lay flat. There was a tremendous explosion and the blast screamed across the ground and I can still remember how the windows of the school seemed to shatter in slow motion. Sometime after this we resumed playing cricket, but our hearts were not in it, particularly as we could hear all the rescue services hurrying to the area.

Mr Eric A. PALMER BROADSTAIRS, Kent.	*Farmer at Eglantine Farm Horton Kirby, nr DARTFORD.*	Reminiscences of V-1's in Horton Kirby area.

The first doodlebug I saw came over the top of our house in the middle of the night. I had a searchlight in a field within a 100 yards of my house and they put this up onto it, then all of a sudden I heard them say 'Douse', which meant to put the light out. The next morning I asked the Sergeant if it was one of the new-fangled things the Germans had got that went over last night. He denied it and said it was one of our planes that was in difficulties. We had about eight or nine balloons put in different fields, then the searchlight was moved down to the valley near the river, and A.T.S. girls were sent to man it. One Saturday afternoon a little while after that, another V-1 hit one balloon cable and that stopped it, and it fell over the hill, but the cable fell right over the church roof and did a lot of damage. After this they put little parachutes on the cables, so as soon as they were hit and the cables broke, the parachutes opened and steadied them.

We were threshing a field of corn just below the farm, with a squad of Land Army girls, who were put on the threshing machines that toured different farms. This V-1 hit a balloon and it was coming straight at us, and the poor girls asked where they should go. I told them their only safe place was on the other side of the stack, behind the machine and to trust to luck. So we all got crouched down there and it hit another balloon cable and swung round and landed about a quarter-mile from us, on the other side of the river, just missing a house.

We had just stopped work after planting a field with cabbages; we had got behind some stacks and waited until the 'All Clear' was sounded; it was between 12.00 and 12.30. We could still hear one doodlebug, but we could not spot it at first because we were looking too low - it was up there a terrible height. Then as we watched it, all of a sudden it started to go into a dive, and that was the one that fell at Lewisham, and killed all those people outside Marks and Spencer's and Woolworths. Nearly the last one I saw came down in a field of corn that we had just cut and had it shocked. This doodlebug set fire to the corn but the airmen were very good, as they helped us scramble the sheaves back to stop the fire running through the whole field.

Mrs Janet KOVAC, COLORADO SPRINGS U.S.A.	*Schoolgirl - living at Gillingham.*	V-1's seen during a blackberrying picnic on the Darland Banks.

I lived in Gillingham, Kent during those flying bomb attacks. As my father was Royal Navy we moved from Newcastle back to Gillingham in early 1943 because it seemed Gillingham was safer than a coastal town. My first absolute awareness of the doodlebugs was in the summer of 1944 when I was nine years old. The whole family, Gran Welland, my mum Hilda, my father Frank, brother John and I had gone on a berry picking picnic on a weekend afternoon late in August. We were on the Darland Banks, just to the south east of Chatham and overlooking the broad valley between Chatham and Bluebell Hill, north of Maidstone. The fact that we were relatively surrounded by possible targets meant little to me at that stage of the war.

This first genuine experience with the V-1's was an active one; at least I got quite a bit of exercise out of it! We paused and looked up as the first flying bomb rumbled into our proximity. Then, when it was just to the south of us - SILENCE! We all ran and dived behind the berry bushes as, out of the almost overpowering lack of sound, came a wondrous Krak-Ka-Boom! Over the period of about 45 minutes the first explosion was followed by three more copy-cats as three more V-1's thundered into view from the east. Luckily the bombs were just far enough away, impacting along the route of what is now occupied by the M2 motorway, thus there was no real harm to us. But our picnic acquired a sort of pattern - pick berries; engine noise; run for cover - silence; fall to grass; BLAM!; pick berries again!

Mr Rodney STONE Bathford, BATH.	*Schoolboy visiting aunt in Church Street, Chatham.*	Sheltering from V-1 under kitchen table.

My mother accepted an invitation from her mother-in-law to escape the blitz on Rochester and Chatham in which the Royal Dockyard was the main target, and join her in the relative safety of rural Lincolnshire.

We made regular journeys back to Rochester, and although not more than five-years old at the time, I could return to the exact spot of this incident today. It was during one of our visits to that 'foreign part' which my mother called 'home' that I had my first encounter with the doodlebugs.

We had visited my aunt in Church Street, Chatham and I was playing with my younger brother and my cousin in the back garden, really more like a concreted yard area adjacent to the house and beyond this was a weed-filled patch, through which some potato plants struggled. We were watching a plane flying very high up, which was making a funny 'spluttering' noise. There was a shriek from the house and my aunt appeared, to drag us all inside the kitchen, with a cry of ''It's a doodlebug! Quick, get under the table!'' (this being the officially recommended procedure if there was no air raid shelter).

The ground floor of my aunt's house (it would now be considered a very poor abode) comprised a scullery and a single living room. The table was a stout pine affair, and large enough to accommodate us all - three children, my mother and my aunt. We crouched there as the phuts and splutters reached a crescendo and then began fading away. We were silent, straining our ears for the passing sound. My aunt crept out to look out of the front door. ''It's gone over,'' she said, ''some other poor beggars are going to cop that one.'' I can still remember her words.

We all came out to catch the last glimpse of the doodlebug that went 'phutting' away over the horizon of rooftops and we returned to our play, after a lecture on what to do if we saw or heard another one. We kept a keen watch that day, but it is the only one I recall seeing.

Mrs Molly FRANKLIN, LYNDEN, Ontario. Canada.	*571 HAA(M) Battery A.A Tower Hill, Strood and at Warden Bay, Sheppey.*	Re-deployment of A.T.S. girls with Heavy Ack Ack Bty.

In July 1944 I was an ATS member of the 571st Heavy Anti-Aircraft (Mixed) battery stationed at Tower Hill, Strood, Kent. When the doodlebugs first started to come over we were ordered to the shelter, as nobody knew what they were. However, after the first few days, like everyone else, we soon took little notice of them as they were so frequent; we watched as our fighters tried to catch them. We soon had orders to pack everything on the site as we were to be moved. Within 24 hours we were on our way - rumours abounded!

We girls travelled atop the furniture in the trucks and saw most of Kent pass by. We eventually arrived at Warden Bay on the Isle of Sheppey, where our tents had been put up by the advance party. Talk about moaning! "God forsaken place." "Not a pub in sight." "No Buses." But we had been sent to the coast to intercept the V-1's on their way to London. We certainly had lots to shoot at as they came over steadily day and night. We claimed a few but never knew how many we destroyed as other ack-ack batteries were also nearby.

Mr A.G.DANIELS, SITTINGBOURNE, Kent.	*Lieutenant, The Buffs at Sheerness Dockyard.*	Lack of action by LAA battery to first V1's.

Early on the morning of the 13th June 1944, I was the Duty Officer in charge of the Light Anti-Aircraft Guns (40mm Bofors) deployed to defend Sheerness Dockyard against attack by low flying enemy aircraft.

It was the custom of the Duty Officer to sleep on a camp bed in a room next to the Battery Office where the Duty Telephonist worked. An excited telephonist awakened me with, "Air raid Warning Red," and the news that the Gun Operations Officer had issued the code word 'Diver, Diver, Diver'. So I ordered the guns to 'Take Post'. In accordance with Standing Orders, I unlocked the Battery Office Safe and found an envelope marked 'Top Secret' with 'Diver' written across it.

I opened the envelope and found a copy of the plans of the Buzz Bomb (V-1) Pilotless Aircraft together with operational details. These details clearly showed they flew on a fixed radio bearing. V-1 plots started coming through which I carefully marked on our Operations Map. It soon became clear that the fixed bearing was over Chatham in the direction of London. After about half-an-hour the Brigade Intelligence Officer came on the telephone to enquire if we had opened fire, so I replied in the negative. Another half hour elapsed and then the Staff Captain 'Q' came on the telephone demanding a report on the number of rounds fired, and should he ask the R.A.S.C. to bring up our reserve of ammunition as most of the gun sites in the area were running low. I again replied in the negative.

An hour later the Brigadier himself came on the telephone in angry mood demanding to know why we had failed to open fire. I replied, "Sir, the targets shown by the plots to be passing over your area in Chatham Sheerness is ten miles from Chatham and the Bofors only has a range of 3000 yards." There was an explosion of obvious rage and he slammed down the telephone. Next morning we did open fire at a Buzz Bomb which had strayed off route, but it was just out of range.

Mr Colin ROCHESTER, REGAALE, Ontario Canada.	*Civilian -Schoolboy in Sittingbourne.*	Bus incident en route home to Sheerness.

I lived near Sheerness in 1944 and during that summer I remember while coming home from school on a bus from Sittingbourne, I saw a V.1 coming straight at us on the top of a hill. The bus driver stopped the bus and we fell to the floor; the doodle bug roared over us, missing us by 20-30 feet, and it just kept going. All we on the bus remained lying down a little longer and then off we went again!

One of the Heavy Anti-Aircraft sites in the Medway Area was sited st Fort Borstal, built to defend Chatham and its Dockyard from earlier invasion threats. Royal Artillery gunners and A.T.S. girls served in this H.A.A. (Mixed) Battery.
(Photo. Mrs A Viebahn)

V-1 Vergeltungswaffen (weapon of retaliation) are seen on a factory production line at Nordhausen Concentration Camp. Of the 8,500 flying bombs launched againsy Great Britain, approximately 2,400 reached these shores.
(Photo. via R. Dutton.)

DOVER and EAST KENT

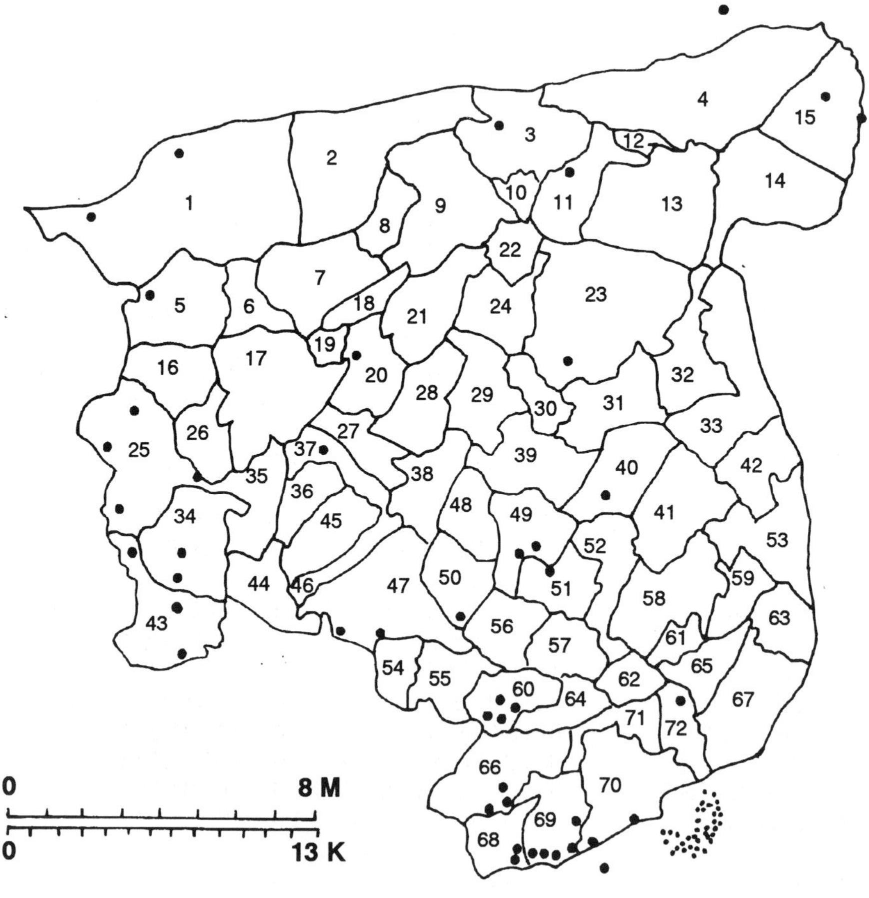

DOVER and EAST KENT

1 WHITSTABLE U.D.	2 HERNE BAY	3 ST. NICHOLAS-AT-WADE
4 BOROUGH OF MARGATE	5 ST. DAMIEN & ST. COSMOS IN THE BLEAN	6 HACKINGTON
7 STURRY	8 HOATH	9 CHISLET
10 SARRE	11 MONKTON	12 ACOL
13 MINSTER-IN-THANET	14 BOROUGH OF RAMSGATE	15 BROADSTAIRS U.D.
16 HARBLEDOWN	17 CITY OF CANTERBURY	18 WESTBERE
19 FORDWICH	20 LITTLEBOURNE	21 WICKHAMBREAUX
22 STOURMOUTH	23 ASH-NEXT-SANDWICH	24 PRESTON
25 CHARTHAM	26 THANNINGTON WITHOUT	27 BEKESBOURNE
28 ICKHAM & WELL	29 WINGHAM	30 STAPLE
31 WOODNESBOROUGH	32 BOROUGH OF SANDWICH	33 WORTH
34 PETHAM	35 UPPER HARDRES	36 BRIDGE
37 PATRIXBOURNE	38 ADISHAM	39 GOODNESTONE
40 EASTRY	41 NORTHBOURNE	42 SHOLDEN
43 WALTHAM	44 LOWER HARDRES	45 BISHOPSBOURNE
46 KINGSTON	47 BARHAM	48 NONINGTON
49 EASOLE ST.	50 WOMENSWOLD	51 EYTHORNE
52 TILMANSTONE	53 BOROUGH OF DEAL	54 DENTON
55 WOOTON	56 SIBERTSWOLD / SHEPHERDSWELL	57 COLDRED
58 SUTTON	59 RIPPLE	60 LYDDEN
61 WEST LANGDON	62 WHITFIELD	63 RINGWOULD
64 TEMPLE EWELL	65 EAST LANGDON	66 ALKHAM
67 ST. MARGARET AT CLIFFE	68 CAPEL-LE-FERNE	69 HOUGHAM WITHOUT
70 BOROUGH OF DOVER	71 RIVER	72 GUSTON

BRIDGE BLEAN RURAL, BROADSTAIRS URBAN, DEAL BOROUGH, DOVER, BOROUGH and RURAL, EASTRY RURAL, FAVERSHAM, MARGATE, RAMSGATE. SITTINGBOURNE, and WHITSTABLE URBAN C.D DISTRICTS

Key AA = ack-ack fire BB = Barrage Balloon F = Fighter attack

Date	Time	Area	District	Cause	Location/Incident/Damage
JUNE					
16.6	05.00	Sittingbourne	Upchurch		In Bayford Marsh
	10.50		Rodmersham		E of Pinks Farm 1 Sl. Inj.
	23.50	Faversham	Eastling		Divan Wood
25.6	23.22	Sittingbourne		F	
27.6	02.08	Sittingbourne	Newington		Wormdale Farm (unexploded)
28.6	16.57	Margate B	Westgate		Exploded in sea
30.6	15.03	Dover B		F	
JULY					
03.7	05.05	Bridge Blean	Waltham		
	18.35	Faversham	Throwley	F	
06.7	04.53	Sittingbourne	Bredgar	F	Swanton St - Dowsells Bank
07.7	19.15	Sittingbourne	Hartlip		Oak Barn Farm - Queensdown Warren
08.7	23.10	Dover R	Hougham	F	
09.7	20.45	Sittingbourne	Lynsted	F	Dam. to buildings, school and Vicarage 13 Sl. Inj.
10.7	03.10	Broadstairs U		F	3 houses DEM. 40 Ser Dam. 332 Sl. Dam.4 Sl. Inj.
12.7	17.30	Sittingbourne	L. Halstow	F	Callum Hills
15.7	15.36	Faversham	Eastling	F	
	17.34	Sittingbourne	Bredgar	F	1 bungalow DEM. 5 houses Ser. Dam 2 K. 2 Sl. Inj.
16.7	10.17	Margate B			In sea

18.7	03.56	Bridge Blean	Patrixbourne		In orchard, extensive damage to trees, minor damage to houses & Bridge Institute
20.7	04.25	Bridge Blean	Barham		Between Lodge Leas Farm and Beach Down 12 houses Ser. Dam.
22.7	16.56	Sittingbourne		F	Chalk Hole orchard
	20.20	Bridge Blean	Chartham	F	Chartham Hatch - dam. to Council School, and 15 cottages 4 Ser. Inj.25 Sl. Inj.
23.7	09.00	Faversham	Selling	F	
25.7	00.01	Broadstairs U			Empty house on Promenade 1 Sl. Inj.
26.7	14.20	Faversham	Doddington		Frangbury Farm
	14.20		Selling		(same incident as the above?)
27.7	15.11	Dover R	Hougham Without	AA	By R.A.F Regiment
29.7	18.25	Dover B			In sea
	18.26	Dover R	Denton		Exploded in air over Biggin Wood Damage to property, 12 houses in Elham Parish damaged
	18.30	Faversham	Luddenham	F	Luddenham Court Farm, damage to school and old Rectory. 2 Sl Inj.
31.7	15.10	Dover R	Capel	F	Church Farm 30 houses Sl. damaged
	15.15	Bridge Blean	Waltham	F	
	23.15	Eastry R	Monkton		Near St Nicholas at Wade
AUGUST					
01.8	07.00	Eastry R	St Nicholas -at-Wade	F	On Marshes nr Stuart Farm
	15.20	Dover R	Lydden	AA	3 houses slight damage
04.8	01.38	Dover B		AA	In sea
	02.04			AA	In sea
	02.46			AA	In sea
	03.08	Bridge Blean	Littlebourne		8 houses DEM. 100 Sl. Dam St. Vincent's Church and Littlebourne School dam. 1 K. 3 Ser. Inj. 25 Sl. Inj.
	03.21	Whitstable U		AA	14 houses slight damage
	04.25	Bridge Blean	Petham	F	Sl. Dam. to All Saints Church, Petham School and 40 houses
07.8	08.10	Dover B		AA	In sea

09.8	06.34	Dover B		AA	In sea
	06.36			AA	In sea
	06.38			AA	In sea
10.8	04.14	Bridge Blean	Barham	AA	
	04.42	Dover B		F	In sea
	17.50	Dover R	Capel	AA	In air - just off cliff at Capel-le-Ferne
12.8	01.30	Eastry R.D	Eythorne	AA	(C.C Type) at Barfreston
13.8	00.12	Dover B		AA	Lydden Spout Coastal Battery huts DEM.1 Ser. Inj. 4 Sl. Inj.
	06.15	Dover R	Lydden	AA	Wickham Bushes Farm
	06.15	Faversham	Throwley		Farm cottages damaged
	08.10	Dover B		AA	In sea
14.8	04.31	Dover B			In sea
15.8	07.40	Dover B		AA	In sea
	08.20			AA	In sea
	14.15	Dover R	Hougham	AA	Fairview Terrace, 30yds N of Three Horse Shoes PH 3 cottages DEM. 1 Ser. Inj. 1 Sl. Inj.
	18.49	Sittingbourne			Some damage 3 Sl. Inj.
16.8	05.20	Dover B			2 Sl. Inj.
	05.24	Faversham	Doddington		Some damage 3 Sl. Inj.
	05.26	Dover B		AA	In sea
	05.30	Dover R	Guston	AA	(C.C Type)
	05.40	Dover B		AA	In sea
	07.10		Buckland		Elverton Farm, Cottage & P.H. damaged. 1 Sl. Inj.
	09.36			AA	In sea - casualties caused from AA fire 3 Sl. Inj.
	16.45	Sittingbourne	Upchurch	F	Train derailed, Southern Railway mainline bridge over Oak Lane DEM. 8 K. 33 Ser. Inj. 28 Sl. Inj
	17.22	Eastry R	Ash		(C.C Type) Nr Little Knell Farm
	17.40	Dover R	Capel	AA	Some Dam. to Royal Oak PH
	18.30	Bridge Blean	Blean	AA	Denstroude Lane, 1 house DEM. stacks set on fire, some dam. in Whitstable .
	19.10	Sittingbourne	Teynham		Nr Teynham Church
	19.45	Eastry R	Nonington		(C.C Type) Kittington Farm
	20.45	Dover R	Alkham	AA	Some damage
	20.58	Dover B		AA	AA site Folkestone Road 2 Sl. Inj

16.8	21.00	Sittingbourne	Iwade	F	Chetney Marsh
	16.39 - 17.42 Dover Borough				5 Flying Bombs shot down in the sea by AA fire
17.8	07.09	Eastry R	Nonington		In field at Easole Street
	07.12	Faversham	Throwley	F	Field at Belmont
	09.15	Dover R	Alkham		Damage to property
	15.10			AA	
	20.42	Bridge Blean	Waltham		In Denge Wood (W/T Type)
	06.15 - 20.37 Dover Borough				7 Flying Bombs shot down in the sea by AA fire
18.8	06.29	Dover B			2 Flying bombs in sea
19.8	03.20	Dover R	Lydden	F	Bell Farm - some damage
	03.29	Dover B			In sea
	06.39			AA	In sea
	06.00 - 06.00 (20.8) Dover Borough				5 Flying bombs shot down in the sea by AA
20.8	15.00	Dover R		AA	Severe Damage
	15.05	Dover B		AA	In sea
21.8					There were 36 Flying bombs shot down in the sea this day
22.8	05.53	Dover B		F	In sea
23.8	07.58	Dover B		A	In sea
	08.08	Sittingbourne	Tunstall		(C.C Type) 5 houses Ser. Dam. 41 Sl. Dam.2 Sl Inj
	09.20	Bridge Blean	Womenswold		
	20.50	Faversham	Doddington	F	Oakenpole Wood
	21.00		Thannington	F	Iffin Wood
24.8	02.55 - 20.15 Dover Borough				4 Flying bombs shot down in the sea by AA fire
27.8	06.35	Dover B		AA	In sea
	06.41			AA	In sea
28.8	14.35	Faversham	Goodnestone	F	Poplar Hall - extensive damage 1 Sl. Inj.
29.8	16.52	Dover B		AA	Off Admiralty pier
	16.55			AA	Off Admiralty pier
	14.29	Dover R	Hougham Without	AA	Contained leaflets
	17.29	Dover B		AA	Shakespeare Cliff
	18.45	Dover R	Hougham Without	AA	In air over Church Farm

30.8	13.15	Dover B		AA	In sea
31.8	05.53	Whitstable UD		F	Minor damage 1 Ser. Inj. 3 Sl. Inj.
	17.45	Dover R	Hougham Without	AA	Lydden Spout, military casualties 2 Ser. Inj. 2 Sl. Inj.
	05.47 - 17.45	Dover Borough			6 Flying Bombs shot down into the sea by AA fire
SEPTEMBER					
01.9	12.00	Bridge Blean	Chartham	F	nr Waltham/Petham border

W/T TYPE Flying Bomb

In order to check the track and the range of the V-1 missiles, approximately 1 in 10 of them were fitted with small wireless telegraphy sets which were monitored by German radio listening posts.

At the height of the V-1 campaign every available gun was brought out of store to combat the menace. Above: An ancient Lewis machine gun was used on Admiralty Pier Dover, but its effectiveness was negligible. (Photo Mr Ted Poulton)

Mr A.A.FOX, I.S.O BROADSTAIRS, Kent.	*Civilian schoolboy in* *Littlebourne.*	V-1 incident 4.8.44 on Dr Mercer's House.

One V-1 fell on Littlebourne on 4th August 1944 in the early hours of the morning. I was eleven years old at the time and was awakened by the raucous spluttering noise of a flying bomb and my bedroom was filled with a red glow from the flames evacuated by its rather primitive engine. I realised at once what it was and dived under the bed clothes. Seconds later there was a terrific explosion caused, as it transpired, by the flying bomb hitting a tree in the back of Dr Mercer's house, halfway up Littlebourne Hill. We spent the rest of the night in our Morrison shelter - a steel table which could be made into a small bed.

My Father was Chief Special Constable for Littlebourne and when he returned home next morning we learned the dreadful truth. He had rushed to the Doctor's house and helped to carry the Doctor, who was injured in the foot, from his house and also rescue his two children, Bill and Anne who were aged about 9 and 12 at the time. The doctor told my father he thought his wife was dead. My father returned to their house and found her lying on the stairs killed by the blast. He covered her up with a sheet and then set out to account for the other casualties. One man was blown into his garden, Mrs Gasbee had her bedroom window blown in on her; she died a few days later. Those whose houses were damaged were given emergency accommodation in the chapel in Norgate St.

The next day, after local helpers had salvaged what they could from the doctor's house, it collapsed and a new house was built after the war. There was speculation about how the V-1 came to crash without its engine cutting out as was the usual practice, but no possible explanation was forthcoming. Doctor Mercer had served Littlebourne and its surrounding villages for some 40 years and was a well liked and respected member of the community. Mrs Mercer was very popular in the village; it was a tragedy that her life was cut short in this way. Mrs Mercer and Mrs Gasbee are named on the village war memorial, situated next to the porch of Littlebourne Church.

Mr A.R.WEBB, MARGATE, Kent.	*Aero-engine fitter with crash crew at R.A.F. Manston.*	First V-1's, Mosquito 'burned-up', Spitfire unable to catch V1's.

I was stationed at R.A.F Manston as an aero engine fitter working on Spitfires, Lancasters, Mosquitoes and Beaufighters until D-Day. I was transferred to the Crash Crew and stationed, with the Yanks, in the Lodge House alongside the main runway. Our Crash Crew consisted of lads like myself, only 19 years-old. RAF Manston was one of the first crash aerodromes to reach when returning from a night's bombing. One bright day we heard a plane high up in the sky and it sounded like a misfiring engine of an aircraft in trouble. Looking up, we saw what appeared to be a Hurricane travelling very fast. We soon realised that it was not a Hurricane and wondered what on earth was causing that noise. We then spotted a Spitfire following this plane but it appeared not to be able to catch up with it. Not long after this a Mosquito landed with all the camouflage paint burnt off. The report was that the pilot had fired at a plane which completely exploded in front of him and he had flown through the explosion, of course, he had virtually been blown up by a flying bomb, and did not know it.

It wasn't very long before we found out about the 'D's (Doodlebugs). As they came over the sea, the Navy and Army blasted at them, then the Air Force took over and carried on shooting them down, right up to the perimeter of London. I watched Spitfires chasing doodlebugs, even in between the wires of the barrage balloons. It was considered that once they had reached London there was not much point in shooting them down. Our lads soon developed techniques for shooting them down and a great many never reached London. Night time was the worst. So long as you could see the flames of the exhaust, our lads would put them down; but if it was very cloudy - well!

Mr P.E.TAPP, MILSTED, Sittingbourne Kent.	*Schoolboy - working on fruit farm, Southbush Lane, near Rainham.*	Newington Bridge Oak Lane, Upchurch - Train incident.

On the day that this flying bomb fell out of the sky (16.8.44), I was working at a fruit farm, moving ladders for a gang of women picking damsons, (Mesdames White, Whylie, Ware, Clark, Duggan, Reid and Trice) plus a group of their young children, as it was the summer holidays. I was a teenager myself and in my last year at school. It was normal for the Observer Corps at the top of Meresborough Lane to fire a parachute flare to warn of any flying bombs, etc. But what we first heard was the unusual engine noise, plus gunfire, from the direction of Sittingbourne. It came over Hartlip Hill, much lower than normal, with an aeroplane following, firing at it, causing puffs of smoke and sparks to come from the V-1. As it was coming straight at us, we all just stood frozen to the spot like rabbits looking at a stoat. At the last minute it rolled over to the right (the plane had wing-tipped it) and then it crashed onto the railway line with the usual explosion. Large lumps of bricks and concrete crashed around us, and then total silence. The women rushed down their ladders and rounded up the children, to make sure they were all O.K., then began to cry with relief - leaving large black rings round their eyes afterwards, where they had rubbed them with their dirty hands.

Whilst this was taking place, a train was making its way to Sittingbourne, but without its normal load of school children from the local towns. There was a noise that one cannot describe, and then a cloud of dust and smoke. I made my way to the farm yard (Wakeleys Farm?), grabbed my bike and rushed to the scene of the crash. The locomotive had cleared the bridge that had been blown up, and lay on its right hand side, the tender had also gone across the gap. The first carriage and second carriage were stuck up in a V shape in the space of the missing bridge and flames were licking up around the carriages in the gap. The whistle on the engine was going full blast. People were walking along the track, and many were still in the rear carriages, and so I went up the bank and assisted some of the older ladies to get down and also helped them retrieve their luggage. There were many servicemen on the train and they devoted their time to trying to rescue those in the front portion. There were many casualties, I don't know how many, and some were laid out on the grass embankment and covered with coats. The local A.R.P. soon arrived and so did the Police 'Specials' - always a law unto themselves. I was soon told to leave the track and keep out of the way. As I was no longer needed, I made for home, but after this event, I always had a healthy respect for V-1's.

Mr Alan MAJOR, CANTERBURY,Kent.	*Civilian Student* *Printer, Rainham.*	Comments on Oak Lane V-1 incident, etc.

Next day the pilot of the Meteor F.1 jet fighter, came down to the scene of the tragedy and was overcome by what he saw, learning of the deaths he had inadvertently caused. It was stressed that he could not possibly have known the doodlebug would swoop down and dive under the railway bridge as the train came along the line. There were open fields and orchards all round the scene and it could have fallen harmlessly in any of these without killing anyone. It was also pointed out to him that, if he had not brought it down, it might well have carried on to fall in Gillingham, Chatham or Rochester, causing a larger number of deaths. It was just pure bad luck.

Another doodlebug incident was at Hartlip, and in a straight line south of the Oak Lane disaster and within sight of each other, on 22nd August 1944. This V-1 had been carried under the wing of a Heinkel He111 and released over the Thames estuary - Sheppey area, and pointed inland. It had crossed Sheppey, the North Kent marshes and Upchurch, but by the time it had reached Hartlip it was very low. It struck the top of some elm trees near the detached farm cottages known as 'Roman Villas' and fell onto them. This was at night and people were in bed. One woman was killed but her husband, son and daughter survived.

Mr Maurice GILBRAITH, HARTLEPOOL, Cleveland.	*A.B. on H.M.M.L. 445* *21st M.L. Flotilla* *Dover & Ramsgate.*	Incidents in Straits of Dover and Rye Bay.

I was an A.B on board HMML *445* of the 21st Motor Launch Flotilla, and we arrived in Dover from our base in the Orkney Islands in March/April 1944, to be based on the Eastern Arm near the Submarine Pens until August/September 1944, when we moved to Ramsgate. My memories of the V-1's are quite vivid, as we saw one crash into the cliffs while we were going on patrol between Dover and Folkestone, and Ron Goodare, our midships Oerlikon gun gunner hit one, which exploded in mid-air.

While at Dover we were fitted with a small rocket gun that fired parachute flares and sometimes we used to patrol the French coast off Boulogne, with the other seven vessels in the Flotilla. When we saw a V-1 fired from the shore, we would launch a flare to help the fighters patrolling over the Channel to locate them. We saw many shot down and many that were toppled over by the fighters going alongside them and tipping their wings. During one of our escort jobs, a British Ack Ack shell fired at a V-1 near Rye Bay, exploded underneath our ship and it split one of our petrol tanks, so we had to put into Rye to have a new one fitted. The good part for us was the extra leave we had while the repairs were being carried out, and it was smashing going home to the quiet North East after all the shelling and V-1's we'd had in Dover.

Mr Harold COLLYER, Kingsdown, nr DEAL.	*Carpenter and A.F.S. fireman - Walmer.*	Incidents at Dover, Deal & Woodnesborough.

I remember the day that the first V-1s arrived. The A.F.S. had been instructed take precautions: in the event of enemy parachutists being dropped they were to man their nearest standpipe with their hoses and 1 inch diameter nozzles at the ready! I don't know how we would have stood up to a determined parachutist with a machine gun, but he would have had a nasty shock at meeting the high powered water jet from a 1 inch nozzle. However, on the night of the arrival of the V-1's the coded message was received at the Deal Fire Service H.Q., namely that 'Parachutists have landed: stand-by stand pipes', so off we went. I was allocated the stand pipe in Walmer Castle Road and we stood by all the remainder of the night with our hoses and 1 inch nozzles.

On another occasion, I was working on the roof of the tall terrace of houses in Dover, which were replaced by the Gateway Flats after the war. I was perched on the parapet of the roof trying to direct a hose onto an incendiary bomb which was lodged in the roof. On this occasion there had been an air raid previously when high explosives and incendiaries had been dropped. I happened to glance round, and much to my horror, I saw a V-1 flying over the harbour, making straight for me and was going to decapitate me - or so it seemed. In fact it passed harmlessly over my head. On yet another occasion, I was on duty in Deal when I saw a Mustang fighter just off the coastline pull out of a dive behind a V-1 and tip it with its wing. That one crashed at Woodnesborough, demolishing a row of cottages; that was the nearest one to Deal.

Mr Charles HUTCHINS, Sholden, nr DEAL.	*GPO Employee - D.T.N. at Dover Castle Casemates.*	V-1's seen in the Dover area.

On clear nights we went to a little canteen outside the Casemates, (called Calais View Canteen) above Dover's East Cliff, and watched them coming in beyond Folkestone and I would say that 90% were shot down. I heard later that the AA guns used special shells, which had what they called 'proximity fuses'. One strange incident was on a beautiful evening when I was going on duty and the V-1's were coming in over Dover. The ack-ack had shot one or two down, but only scored a near miss on another. This one shot straight up into the summer sky - up and up it went, whilst we on the ground thought that it would explode any minute, but it didn't, it just continued on its upward flight till I could stay no longer as duty called.

Mrs H.A SANDYS, ULVESTON, Cumbria.	*WRNS - based at HMS 'Wasp' and Boys County School.*	Incidents at Dover and St Margaret's Bay.

I was stationed in Dover from September 1943 until June 1945, and remember the Buzz Bombs all too well. Three episodes stand out in my mind. The day I stood at the window of my 'cabin' in the Boy's County School, it had originally been the art room of the school, and was the top right hand window. I became mesmerized as I watched a Buzz Bomb come winging its way at eye level towards the school. I was convinced it would come right through the windows! I flung myself on the floor, and then saw a rocket, fired by the crew manning the gun on the ridge by the school, just clear the wing by six feet.

Standing on the cliffs between Dover and St Margaret's Bay and seeing an enormous flare on the French coast (the launching of a doodlebug), watching this Buzz Bomb skim over the sea, its rear flame reflecting in the water, and then seeing it shot down and all in the space of about ten minutes.

One incredibly clear day I was invited to go into one of the gun emplacements that had been established to shoot down V-1's, as I walked down the Old Folkestone Road into Dover. The crew loaned me a pair of binoculars and I could see a German troop train slowly puffing its way north, also the sunlight glancing off the windscreens of vehicles.

Mr J.W.HUSSEY, SANDWICH, Kent.	*Civilian - Apprentice* *D.C.R.E. electrician.*	A.T.S. Girl incident; V-1 relic at Alkham.

I was an apprentice electrician attached to the D.C.R.E. and 17 yrs old at the time. During the month of June 1944 I was working at Don 8, an ack-ack battery above Folkestone, situated along Crete Road East, when the action alarm for approaching enemy aircraft, in this case the doodlebugs, was sounded. A hit was made on one wing of a Bug, causing an erratic and dangerous flight, being observed by all those present, who dived for cover. But the A.T.S. girl listening on the range finder 'carried on' - until an officer pulled her down with the remark, "Get down, you silly bitch!"

The Doodle Bug exploded in a wooded area near Alkham Bottom, where for some years after the ball of iron used as a balance in this flying bomb was to be seen at an entrance to one of the houses. After the action, the ATS girl got up, saluted the officer and said, "Sir, bloody I may be, stupid at times, but I am not a bitch!" I have often wondered since if that brave girl survived the war?

Mr Armine HARELY, Costessey, NORWICH.	*R.A.F Regiment at* *Lydden Spout, near* *Dover.*	V-1 diverted onto American AAA camp.

When we first moved into the area we were either at Hythe or Dymchurch. After a while we moved onto a rifle range between Folkestone and Dover, on the cliff tops, where a Hispano cannon almost tottered on the edge of the cliff. We were sent next to a long-range artillery gun, set in the cliff; it fired on German 'E' boats in the Channel. We used a track almost opposite a pub called The Plough, which was on the coast road, to get down into Dover.

A battery of American 90 mm ack-ack guns 'set up shop' behind us. They had come straight off a boat at Liverpool, and had some wonderful equipment, and coffee on tap all day long. We couldn't compete with them on equipment, neither could our N.A.A.F.I. wagon, especially when we saw two female U.S.A. film stars serving on their P.X. truck. Their four guns fired all together, as they were being directed from a truck with a radar (SCR 584) dish on it.

Normally a doodlebug would go up in a cloud of smoke and fire, but on one occasion a V-1 veered away over Folkestone, then it turned back towards where we were, as it seemed to be drawn by a magnet. It crashed right in the middle of their camp, luckily only three of them had to go back home injured.

Mr John WILLSON, ASH-next-Sandwich Kent.	*Civilian - ATC Cadet with No 1859 Squadron ATC - living at Ash.*	V-1's plotted for the Eastry R.D.C. Civil Defence H.Q.

The first night that the V-1's came over some senior members (I was 17 1/2 years old) of 'C' Flight 1895 Sqd Air Training Corps volunteered to go to the searchlight site at Foxborough Hill, Woodnesborough. This searchlight was one of the biggest ones around, mounted on four wheels and was connected to some huge sound locators, also mounted on wheels, that automatically homed it onto a target - all very technical for that time. We had a plotting board, which was a circular piece of wood about the size of a dart board, on which was the Ordnance Survey map of our area, all marked up with National Grid lines. Our orders were to phone in Grid reference numbers, giving the direction of the explosions and the estimated distance, by counting the seconds between seeing a flash to hearing the noise. But as there were many flashes at night, without an explosion to hear, things tended to get a bit complicated. We also had an old shepherd's hut on wheels, with a couple of camp beds inside and the idea was that we could sleep there when nothing was going on - what a hope. To us lads this was 'the real thing' and so who wanted to sleep inside that hut - anyway, it had fleas in it!

When we arrived there was great excitement with all the searchlight crew standing by with rifles and fixed bayonets, even a chap from the cookhouse had his rifle with him. There were also some R.A.F Regiment chaps there with Bren guns, and they also had some of the Hispano 30mm Cannons. We had to go on duty at 19.00 hrs, but had to wait until after midnight before anything started to happen so it was a bit of an anti-climax at first. All anybody had been told was that the Germans were planning to send over some sort of new weapon that night, but no one had any idea what this was, what it looked like, or even what it would do, so everyone was very cautious. I was there with Alf Tidy, who came from Wingham, and Roy Caspell from Worth, another Wingham chap named Clark and some others. I do remember having a terribly dry throat, and suddenly wanting to go to the toilet when I saw that first V-1 coming. However, by the time the first Buzz Bombs started to come over there were lots of low clouds drifting across from Sandwich Bay over the top of the hill, so all we could see were these twinkling lights passing over above it.

Mr Ovenden (Home Guard), who lived nearby, came out in uniform with his rifle, and everybody started firing away at these Buzz Bombs, together with the Bren guns and the Hispano cannons, so the amount of noise was terrific. However, it was soon decided that we were to get down into the trench shelter, and we were able to observe from a somewhat safer distance. The Sergeant promised, "I'll keep you informed, if we're still here"! Their searchlight was off and on all the time, but the cloud was so low, it was just like 'lighting-up a brick wall' with the beam just like driving into a bank of fog with your headlights on. As the V-1's went over they were only a hundred or so feet up; and we could see the flames coming out the back, but could not pick out their silhouettes.

We started plotting the explosions onto our gridded map and sending these plots back to the Eastry C.D. HQ, which was near the railway crossing at Sandwich. I think that we were sending back this information so that the local C.D. Heavy Rescue Squads could be sent out to deal with any damage or casualties.

Sailors and WRNS at the 'Calais View Canteen' - a Nissen hut on the cliff side at Dover Castle from where they watched V-1's crossing the Channel. (Photo via Mrs Joyce Atkinson)

Reporting V-1 launches while on patrol in mid-Channel HMML446 had the distinction of shooting down at least one flying bomb with her midships 30mm Oerlikon cannon. Gunner Ron Goodare is ready to take on any more in sight! (Photo Mr M. Gilbraith)

These ATS girls manning a predictor for a Heavy A.A battery at Pegwell Bay near Ramsgate were tumbling out of their beds before first light - hence their leather waistcoats to ward off early morning chills.
(Photo via Mrs Joy Williams)

FOLKESTONE, HYTHE and ELHAM

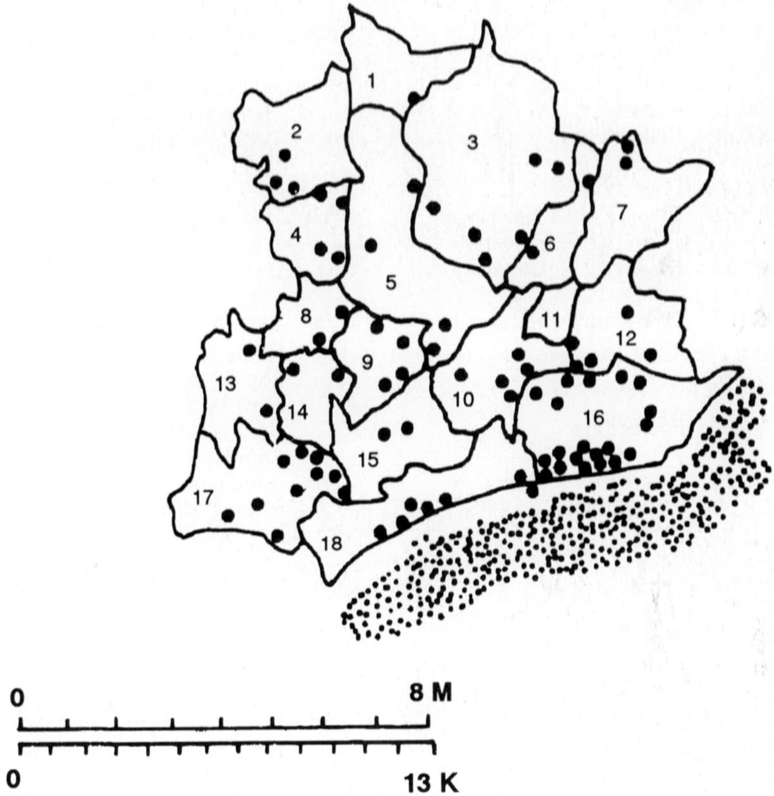

1 STELLING MINNIS	2 ELMSTED	3 ELHAM
4 STOWTING	5 LYMINGE	6 ACRISE
7 SWINGFIELD	8 MONKS HORTON	9 POSTLING
10 NEWINGTON	11 PADDLESWORTH	12 HAWKINGE
13 SELLINDGE	14 STANFORD	15 SALTWOOD
16 BOROUGH OF FOLKESTONE	17 LYMPNE	18 BOROUGH OF HYTHE

ELHAM RURAL, FOLKESTONE and HYTHE BOROUGH C.D DISTRICTS

Key AA = ack-ack fire F = Fighter attack

Date	Time	Area	District	Cause	Location/Incident/Damage
JUNE					
16.6	00.17	Hythe			Hythe Ranges 1 Sl. Inj
	10.40	Folkestone		AA	Windows damaged
17.6	03.48	Folkestone		AA	
	15.10	Elham	Hawkinge	F/AA	
25.6	23.12	Elham	Stowting	F	
27.6	00.24	Folkestone	Sandgate		Exploded in air over Castle Road
	01.12			AA	Exploded in air
	01.19			AA	Exploded in air
	01.30	Folkestone		AA	Near R.A.S.C Barracks Shorncliffe
	02.20	Elham	Sellindge		Hoddifers Farm
	02.30	Folkestone			In sea
30.6	16.35	Elham	Monks Horton	F	
	22.13	Folkestone		AA	Nr Cheriton Rectory 5 Sl. Inj.
JULY					
03.7	15.30	Folkestone		AA	Denmark Street, 9 houses and 1 P.H DEM. 18 houses 2 P.H's part DEM.42 houses, 8 shops badly Dam. 800 houses & 40 shops slight Dam. 3 K. 8 Ser. Inj. 47 Sl. Inj.
	17.15	Elham	Saltwood	F	
	22.44		Lyminge	F	Extensive dam. to houses 12 Sl.Inj.
07.7	12.25	Elham	Elmsted	F	Evington Park
	17.32		Stowting	F	Lymbridge Green
10.7	20.08	Hythe		F	5 Sl. Inj.
16.7	04.24	Elham	Lympne	F	
	04.28		Elham	F	Mill Down
	12.38		Postling	F	

19.7	03.04	Folkestone		AA	In sea
	08.40	Elham	Newington	AA	4 houses Dam. 1 Ser. Inj. 1 Sl. Inj
20.7	23.35	Hythe			In sea
21.7	00.44	Hythe		AA	In sea
	12.05	Folkestone			
22.7	23.58	Elham	Acrise	AA	
23.7	04.50	Hythe		AA	Dilgate
	09.40	Elham	Elmsted	F	Little Pett Bottom Farm
	14.24		Lympne	AA	Damaged over sea and crashed at Otterpool Lane 20 houses dam. Service huts and tents destroyed 1 K. 7 Ser. Inj 10 Sl. Inj
24.7	01.50	Elham	Newington	AA	Damage to buildings
	23.08	Hythe		AA	South of town
26.7	04.38	Hythe		AA	Over sea
	06.20	Elham	Saltwood		Home Farm, Sandling extensive damage to buildings 2 Sl. Inj.
	14.10	Folkestone	Sandgate	AA	Exploded in air
	14.12	Hythe		AA	Over sea
	23.54			AA	South of town
27.7	01.10	Hythe		AA	NW of town
	01.10			AA	South of town
	01.13			AA	SE of town
	01.17			AA	SE of town
	15.25	Elham	Lympne	AA	1 Sl. Inj.
	16.44		Lyminge	F	
	17.00		Sellindge		Damage to 20 houses
	17.40		Lympne	F	
	19.20	Hythe		AA	In air W of town
	22.45	Folkestone		F	Shorncliffe Road Extensive damage 3 Ser. Inj. 6 Sl. Inj.
	23.55	Hythe		AA	2 Flying bombs SW of town
	23.59			AA	SE of town
28.7	00.03	Hythe		AA	SE of town
	13.25	Elham	Saltwood		Thorne Wood
	13.30	Hythe		AA	In air S of town
	22.30	Elham	Lympne		
	22.36	Hythe		AA	Over foreshore

29.7	00.31	Hythe		AA	S of town
	14.10			AA	2 Flying bombs SE of town
	18.27	Elham	Saltwood	F	Nr Stone Farm
	18.30	Hythe		AA	2 Flying bombs over sea
	18.35	Folkestone	Sandgate	AA	exploded in air
	19.15	Elham	Hawkinge		Dane Farm
	21.30	Hythe		AA	In sea S of town
	23.00			AA	4 Flying bombs, 3 in sea 1 NE of town
	23.01	Elham	Stanford	AA	Hope Farm
	23.30	Folkestone	Sandgate	F	
	23.44			AA	In sea
30.7	00.55	Hythe		AA	In air E of town
31.7	07.35	Elham	Lyminge	F	
	16.36		Lympne	F	
AUGUST					
03.8	00.41	Hythe		AA	In sea
	01.47	Hythe	Oathill	AA	Exploded in air
	02.30			AA	In sea
	04.52			AA	In sea
	05.45	Elham	Etchinghill		AA
	12.31		Hawkinge	AA	Between Gibraltar & Dane Farms. RAF buildings dam. at airfield 2 RAF Sl Inj
	01.41 - 23.59				10 Flying bombs shot down into sea by AA & 3 by fighters off Folkestone
04.8	01.23	Elham	Lympne	AA	
	01.25	Folkestone			
	02.04	Hythe		AA	
	02.25			AA	
	18.20	Folkestone	Sandgate		Nr Royal Kent Hotel, dam. to property
	00.10 - 20.14				17 Flying Bombs shot down in the sea by AA fire off Hythe
	01.19 - 20.14				20 Flying Bombs shot down by AA fire 8 by fighters into the sea off Folkestone
05.8	17.10	Elham	Sellindge		Stone Hill, 2 houses Dem. 3 Ser.Inj 3 Sl. Inj
	02.30 - 17.00				8 Flying bombs shot down in sea by AA & 2 by fighters off Folkestone
	00.25 - 05.58				8 Flying bombs shot down in the sea off Hythe 7 by AA fire

06.8	04.30 - 07.01				2 Flying bombs shot down in sea by AA; 4 by fighters off Folkestone
	04.35 - 18.57				4 Flying bombs shot down in sea by AA fire off Hythe
07.8	01.35	Folkestone		AA	In sea
	07.25	Elham	Monks Horton	F	Priory Lane
	07.45		Elmsted	F	Little Pett Bottom
	08.06		Hawkinge		Swingfield Minnis, Reinden Wood dam. to RAF huts
	10.50	Folkestone		AA	In air over Ross Barracks, Shorncliffe
	07.26 - 10.53				6 Flying bombs shot down in sea by AA fire off Hythe
08.8	06.10	Folkestone			Foreland Ave, 12 houses DEM 100 Ser Dam1 Ser.Inj. 7 Sl. Inj.
09.8	06.45	Folkestone		AA	In sea, blast damage caused to 200 buildings
	06.31 - 06.40				4 Flying bombs shot down in sea by AA fire off Folkestone
10.8	04.45	Hythe	Hythe		1 house DEM many damaged 1 K. 8 Sl. Inj.
	17.45	Elham	Lympne	AA	(C.C Type) 2 Sl. Inj.
	21.30		Hawkinge	F	The Firs Farm, Elham Rd Did not explode
	04.05 - 21.30				4 Flying bombs shot down into sea by AA & 2 by fighters off Folkestone
	04.45 - 21.29				3 Flying bombs shot down into sea by AA & 1 by fighter off Hythe
11.8	07.31	Elham	Elham	AA	Slight damage 2 Sl. Inj.
	14.05	Folkestone		AA	Exploded in the air, 13 shops 30 hotelson sea front & in Guildhall Street dam.
	14.05	Hythe		AA	In sea
	14.07			F	In sea
	14.10			AA	In sea
	7.21 - 14.09				5 Flying bombs shot down in sea by AA fire off Folkestone
12.8	01.40	Folkestone		AA	Nos 21 & 23 Grimston Gardens DEM. Widespread damage 1 Sl. Inj.
	03.15	Elham	Lympne	AA	In Aldergate Wood

12.8	01.20 - 06.15				7 Flying Bombs shot down in sea by AA fire off Folkestone
	01.33 - 03.11				4 Flying bombs shot down in sea by AA fire off Hythe
13.8	01.10	Folkestone		AA	In sea
	06.10			AA	In sea
	06.12	Hythe		AA	Damage to farmhouse and 2 cottages
	07.45				(V-1 fitted with a cable cutter) *
14.8	01.43 - 04.30				8 Flying Bombs shot down in sea by AA off Folkestone
	04.02 - 07.01				8 Flying bombs shot down in sea by AA fire off Hythe
15.8	04.20	Elham	Stanford	AA	
	04.30		Acrise	AA	Near Winter Down Farm
	14.10	Hythe		AA	Earlsfield Road, 5 houses DEM, 500 houses damaged, much blast damage. 5 K. 5 Ser Inj. 12 Sl. Inj
	18.06	Folkestone	Sandgate	AA	Exploded in air, damage to houses
	08.56 - 18.45				15 Flying bombs shot down in sea by AA off Folkestone
	14.25 - 18.43				7 Flying Bombs shot down in sea by AA fire off Hythe
16.8	07.10	Elham	Hawkinge	AA	Dane Farm, slight damage
	08.40		Lympne	AA	Newingreen, exploded in air 12 Houses damaged
	09.40	Folkestone		AA	In air over Dinton Road
	17.39	Elham	Postling	AA	Nr Postling Church 2 Sl. Inj.
	20.58		Newington	AA	
	05.18 - 09.59				12 Flying Bombs shot down in sea by AA off Folkestone
	05.20 - 21.20				30 Flying Bombs shot down in sea by AA & 6 by fighters off Hythe
17.8	06.30	Folkestone		AA	Exploded in air
	13.19	Elham	Elham	AA	Standard Hill Farm
	16.20	Hythe			100 houses Slight Damage 3 Sl. Inj.
	20.35	Folkestone Boro		AA	Wear Bay Crescent - widespread damage to property 4 Ser. Inj. 3 Sl. Inj.
	06.09 - 20.41				27 Flying Bombs shot down in sea by AA & 1 by fighter off Folkestone

17.8	13.22 - 20.41				16 Flying Bombs shot down in sea by AA off Hythe
18.8	00.06 - 07.24				6 Flying bombs shot down in sea by AA off Folkestone
	06.56 - 07.25				5 Flying Bombs shot down into sea by AA fire off Hythe
19.8	03.10	Folkestone		AA	In sea
	03.18			AA	In sea
	03.28			AA	In sea
	06.41	Elham	Lyminge	F	Stowting Rough Wood
	06.50	Folkestone		AA	Exploded in air above the SouthernRailway Pier - blast damage to houses and property 1 Ser. Inj.
	14.30			AA	In sea near Southern Railway Pier. Blast damage from Fishmarket to No 17 Wear Bay Crescent 1 Ser. Inj 4 Sl. Inj
	06-00 (19.8) - 06.00 (20.8)				18 Flying Bombs shot down in sea by AA off Folkestone and 19 shot down off Hythe by AA
	03.15 - 06.58				12 Flying Bombs shot down in sea by AA off Hythe
20.8	14.43	Folkestone		AA	In sea - minor blast dam.3 Sl. Inj
	06.05 - 16.41				8 Flying Bombs shot down in sea by AA & 2 by fighters off Folkestone
	15.45 - 16.44				4 Flying Bombs shot down in sea by AA off Hythe
21.8	02.12 - 20.54				13 Flying Bombs shot down in sea by AA & 3 by fighters off Folkestone
	02.16 - 20.25				18 Flying Bombs shot down in sea by AA off Hythe
22.8	07.32	Elham	Acrise		Winter Down Farm
	03.25 - 07.43				8 Flying Bombs shot down in sea by AA fire off Folkestone
	06.00 (22.8) - 06.00 (23.8)				20 Flying Bombs shot down in sea by AA off Hythe
23.8	08.20	Elham	Elham	F	20 houses and farm buildings damaged, Railway line blocked
	08.25		Acrise	AA	20 houses blast damage, 1 Sl. Inj.
	09.06		Lyminge	AA	20 houses blast damage

23.8	20.44	Hythe		AA	Four Flying bombs in sea
	20.48			AA	In sea
	20.50			AA	In sea
	06.00 (22.8) - 06.00 (23.8)				14 Flying Bombs shot down in sea by AA & 1 by a fighter off Folkestone
	06.00 (22.8) - 06.00 (23.8)				20 Flying Bombs shot down in sea by AA & 4 by fighters off Hythe
	07.48 - 20.52				12 Flying bombs shot down in the sea by AA & 1 by a fighter off Folkestone Borough
24.8	06.25	Elham	Postling		Cuckoo Lane
	18.15		Elmsted	F	Bodsham - 20 houses damaged
	18.41		Paddlesworth		In air over village - slight damage to 3 houses
	19.43		Stelling Minnis	AA	Slight damage to 15 houses 2 Sl. Inj.
	02.40 - 21.15				33 Flying Bombs shot down in the sea by AA; 4 by fighters off Folkestone
	02.47 - 21.15				32 Flying Bombs shot down in the sea by AA 4 by fighters off Hythe (In addition 83 Flying Bombs shot down in sea)
25.8	07.04	Folkestone		AA	In sea
27.8	06.30 - 06.51				9 Flying Bombs shot down in the sea by AA off Folkstone
	06.40 - 07.23				9 Flying Bombs shot down in the sea by AA off Hythe
28.8	14.05 - 19.25				22 Flying Bombs shot down in the sea by AA off Hythe
	14.20 - 19.26				36 Flying Bombs shot down in the sea by AA off Folkestone
29.8	16.56	Elham		AA	Slight damage 1 Sl. Inj
	17.30	Folkestone		F	(contained leaflets)
	12.07 - 23.32				32 Flying Bombs shot down in the sea by AA 2 by fighters off Folkestone
	13.06 - 23.21				26 Flying bombs shot down in the sea by AA off Hythe

30.8	08.23	Elham	Elmsted		Whatsole Street Farm damaged
	00.08 - 13.10				10 Flying Bombs shot down in the sea by AA off Folkestone
31.8	02.06	Folkestone		F	
	04.20			AA	
	04.25	Hythe		AA	In sea
	05.46	Elham	Lyminge		Considerable damage to Methodist Church & Church Rd. 150 houses dam 9 Sl. Inj
	08.40		Monks Horton	AA	Nr Hempton Lodge 3 Sl. Inj.
	09.59	Folkestone		AA	In Brockman Road, 13 houses DEM. 500 damaged 6 Ser. Inj. 49 Sl. Inj.
	11.35	Elham	Hawkinge	F	Slight damage to 3 aircraft, RAF huts and control van 1 Sl. Inj.
	12.14	Folkestone		AA	1 house DEM, 6 Severe dam. 2 Sl Inj
	12.40	Hythe		AA	8 houses Sl. Damaged 1 Sl. Inj
	05.41 - 17.42				19 Flying Bombs shot down in the sea by AA; 3 by fighters off Folkestone
	05.49 - 10.40				9 Flying Bombs shot down into the sea by AA off Hythe . (In addition there were 3 more Flying Bombs shot down into the sea)

ANTI AIRCRAFT DEFENCES

The significant increase in the numbers of V-1's shot down off the coastal strip between Dungeness and Dover was due to the redistribution of anti-aircraft guns of all kinds from the 'Gun Belt' around South London to the coast.

CABLE CUTTERS

* *In an attempt to defeat the balloon barrage around London, a saw-toothed cable cutter was introduced to the leading edge of V-1 wings to slice through the steel cables tethering the balloons to their winches.*

A photograph of a stricken V-1 was taken by a Daily Express photographer from a window in Cheriton Road, Folkestone on 31st August; the office of Joe Chandler, a taxi proprietor.
(Photo Mr. J. Chandler via Roy Humphreys.)

In August 1944 all the available ack-ack guns were repositioned along the coast of Kent and Sussex between Littlehampton and Deal to engage the V-1's approaching the coast, including this 40mm Bofors on the cliffs at Capel.
(Photo via Roy Humphreys.)

Mr D.E.LLEWELLYN, GEORGETOWN, Ontario Canada.	*Pilot - with No 74 Sqd flying Spitfire* LF *IX from Lympne.*	Tempest accidentally shot down nr Lympne.

In May 1944, No 74 Sqd commenced operations from Lympne flying the Mark LF IX Spitfires. Some of the boys had been having a night out in Folkestone the night that the first Doodle-bugs were launched. We had no idea what they were. I remember hitching a ride back to Lympne on the back of a motorcycle, driving along the coast road with red tracer from Bofors guns streaming out to sea. The tale-tell red glow of the rocket exhaust was not evident that night, perhaps they were in cloud.

It was soon evident that the flight path of the doodlebugs from one particular launch pad passed directly overhead, but we were incensed that we were not allowed to go up after them. The Spitfire IX was considered too slow and the Tempest and the Spitfire Mark XIV squadrons were the ones used to combat the V-1, although a number of Wing Commanders and Squadron Leaders ignored these rules, and went up freelance. Naturally we, and the other squadrons on the Wing, complained.

The day our complaints paid off I was, as 'B' Flight Commander, designated to lead the Squadron that day. We were suddenly told we could send up an 'anti Diver' patrol of two aircraft for the last hour of the daylight 'Readiness'. I took Sgt. Dalgell as my partner. I had a nasty suspicion that the controllers might favour the more regular patrols, so we ignored their instructions, until they put us on to one which was directed (as we expected) over Lympne. As we approached from the west it was crossing from right to left at our height, just below the cloud level (about 4,000 ft, I think). Because they were supposed to be fast, I pulled up into the cloud, did a 90° turn and came down directly behind it with speed, lined it up and fired.

At that moment one of those damned 'free-lance' Tempests came up from below, right in front of me, and I hit him in both wings, directly above Lympne. (Pieces of aircraft fell on the field and were shown to me afterwards). Since I could do nothing about the Tempest, I went on and shot down the doodlebug. It turned over to the left and went into a field somewhere to the north of Lympne. When I later phoned to say I had accidentally shot down a Tempest, a bored WAAF said, "Oh, what, another one?" and rang off. It did not matter anyway. The Tempest was flown by the NEWCHURCH Wing-Commander, and there were far too many

Tempests (and Wing Commanders!) floating around in everybody's way, in June 1944!

The entry in my logbook reads:-
June 29 Spitfire IX 'N' ANTI DIVER PATROL 1.00 HR
also the unauthorised comment (we all did it)
1 Doodle Bug destroyed , 1 Tempest damaged
On July 5th we left Lympne.

Mr Brian SHERRAN, DEAL, Kent.	*R.A.F. Construction Unit -* *Marsh ALG's.*	Incidents at Hawkinge comments on attackers.

I was based at Hawkinge, in billets, and used to travel around the Romney Marsh checking my detachments in that area. The first we heard were rumours from the Tempest squadrons that they had met an aircraft which they thought was piloted, but didn't know, and they had chased it as far as Maidstone, but they had had to turn back as they couldn't keep up with it, but we were not told anything officially. The next time was about three or four days later. I was billeted just outside Hawkinge and it was about 10.00pm when I heard, what I thought was a German aircraft, a very deep engine note, and saw a light which I took to be a searchlight, we didn't know it was the engine. This thing came over Hawkinge and may have been 200 ft up, straight over my billet and I was just shattered. Nobody tried to attack it, of course it wasn't taking evasive action. It seemed that all through that night they were coming over and it wasn't until morning that we all saw what they were. I remember it was a misty sort of day and these things were coming in fairly low under the cloud base and were leaving the Spitfires and everything else right behind, it was really worrying. What we did find was, being some 80 miles from London, that leave detachments were kept back at weekends away from their families. People who had been on leave would come back with dreadful stories of what a lot of damage they had seen in London, and upset all the others.

We found that practically everybody underestimated their speed, as quite a number of times I saw with Spitfires and Tempests, and whenever the ack-ack opened up while they were chasing the V-1's; I have never seen a shell burst in front of a V-1! The other thing at this time was that there were Tempests upside down in cornfields, in dykes and so on. At the beginning they were just going flat out all the time they were in the air and so their engines just wore out in a matter of weeks. That is why they started standing patrols later on. I can remember one case at Hawkinge, seeing a very sick doodlebug that couldn't get away from anything. The planes were not allowed to attack them over the town of Folkestone, so there were numerous planes all circling round it; even an Air Sea Rescue Walrus amphibian, waiting for it to fly clear of the built-up area. As soon as it did, you couldn't tell who got it first!

Mr Ernest CARTWRIGHT, Woolston, SOUTHAMPTON.	*WO/AG No 277 A.S.R. Sqd based at Hawkinge.*	Incidents at Hawkinge and off Dungeness.

I joined No 277 Sqd in January 1944, and the aircraft we flew were Spitfire V's and Walrus amphibian, as a crew member of the latter type I took part in several rescues. One night, when sleeping in the Crew Room at Dispersal, I recall hearing an almighty bang and the next morning, when we went outside, finding the tail section of a V-1 lying at the dispersal between two of our aircraft. I also remember standing outside our crew room one day, and watching a V-1 approaching over Folkestone with a Tempest diving after it. The Tempest opened fire, hitting the V-1, and then it flew straight through the explosion. We fully expected to see the Tempest in trouble, but she flew serenely on; all in a day's work for those boys!

My log book notes that on 24th August 1944 we picked up a Flight Lieutenant Collier of No 91 Sqd. We were later informed that he was the first pilot to bring down a doodlebug by tipping it with his wing, after running out of ammunition. During this period, aircraft flying below a certain height were only allowed to fly out to sea in certain places, namely Dungeness and North Foreland, but the ack-ack gunners were inclined to be a little 'trigger' happy. As I remember, one day we crossed the coast at Dungeness and then proceeded to fly up the coast at, what we had thought, was a safe distance from the shore. There was also quite a heavy mist hanging over the sea, and then suddenly we saw these little explosions around us, much too close for comfort. The sound of the Walrus engine was quite distinctive and not unlike a V-1. This episode taught us a valuable lesson!

Mr R.C.MCKENZIE, MEDICINE HAT, Alberta Canada.	*Private - Canadian infantry billeted in Folkstone.*	First Folkestone V-1? shot-down by Spitfire.

I served in the Canadian infantry (Calgarry Highlanders) during the war and in June 1944, my regiment was billeted in the empty seafront hotels, in Folkestone. It was a pleasant June afternoon, and several of us were standing about the front entrance to our hotel when one of the first doodlebugs we ever saw came flying towards us across the Channel. The spluttering and popping noise of the damned things drew all our eyes to it. It wasn't very high up when, just as it got almost directly overhead, a Spitfire suddenly dived out from the clouds above the Buzz Bomb and fired a short burst at it, from very close quarters. As soon as the bullets struck there was a horrendous explosion. The last thing I saw before I was blown backwards into the Hotel lobby was the Spitfire being flipped into a backward loop by the terrific blast.

Luckily, although we were all shaken up, not one of us witnessing this little drama, was badly hurt, even though there was a lot of glass from the shattered windows flying about. I've often wondered if the Spitfire and the pilot managed to survive. I very much doubt it. Of course, from then on, many Buzz Bombs came over Folkestone and Dover areas, but this was my first encounter with one and I strongly believe this was the first Doodlebug to appear over Folkestone, as we were right on the waterfront and would have heard or seen any others.

Mr H.A.SANSUM, SUTTON-on-SEA, Lincs.	*Gunner - LAA Regt. based at West Hougham.*	Incident of leaflet-carrying V-1.

I joined the 59th Territorial Regiment Heavy Anti-Aircraft Brigade prewar, but at this time I had been seconded to an L.A.A. Battery and we had been ordered to a place between Folkestone and Dover. The site was a field on the left side of the main road coming from Folkestone, (at West Hougham) so we were facing in the direction of Dover. We were camped in this field, and before our guns had been put in position, a number of these Flying Bombs came over Dover, and the Heavy Ack-Ack opened up and we were watching the bursts from their shells. Suddenly one of the flying bombs banked over to its left and then the engine cut out. I could see that it was coming towards us - it came lower and lower and I thought that it was going to land amongst us. I got on the ground and put my tin hat on and I was still watching this bomb, as it continued to come directly for us, getting lower and lower all the time. I tried very hard to get inside my tin hat. Suddenly a puff of wind hit the Flying Bomb and it banked to the left again, and it hit a rise in the next field to us and exploded - exactly opposite where we were laying.

I got up and ran across the field we were in, across the road and across the other field to the scene of the explosion. I got there very quickly, but there was an Army cook already there. I was very surprised, where he came from I don't know, as I had thought that we were the only AA battery around there. However I was looking for some souvenirs and there were a lot of papers about the place, obviously blown from the bomb, but there were also some rolls of thick cardboard with some papers inside them. Some of these rolls had split open so I picked up a few of the least damaged ones, and one undamaged roll, and went back to our gun site. When I got back a lot of my colleagues wanted some of these papers so I started giving them around. Then a sergeant arrived in a great hurry and ordered me to go over to the Battery Office. When I arrived there one of the officers was in a state and, by the way that he spoke to me, I thought that I was going to be put in the 'glass house'. So I had to hand over all the pamphlets, but he did say I could keep one of them - which I have done for years.

Mr J.V. REILLY,	*Air Ministry Wireless Op*	Incidents near
HYTHE. Kent.	*at Lympne D/F station.*	R.A.F Lympne.

I vividly remember the summer of 1944, and the first night the V-1 came over. I was on duty at our Adcock D/F station at Court-at-Street and we were somewhat mystified by the strange 'aircraft engine' noises that we could hear in the distance. By the time that it was daylight we still had not received the usual 'all clear' message, but shortly after taking down our blackout shutters we saw our first doodlebug - a black evil-looking object, making an incredible racket from its flame-belching, rear mounted, engine. We were to become very familiar with this rather scary sound in the ensuing months, and I counted as many as fourteen one evening from a viewpoint on The Roughs overlooking the Romney Marsh.

One other hair-raising incident happened to one colleague of mine when on his way to post a letter in a pillar box near to his home in Berwick

Lane, Lympne. He heard a loud swishing noise and, on looking up, he saw this large black object no more than 20 feet above his head. He told me that he could actually see the welding on its bodywork, but had no time to do anything but throw himself in the ditch. It came down only about 400 yards from where he lay, near an R.A.F. Regiment ack-ack gun site, killing two airmen. Incidentally, the blast from this particular explosion blew everything off our Dining Room table (we had been advised at this time to leave our windows open), where my wife and I were sitting having breakfast. I have a distinct recollection of spilt milk and Puffed Wheat all over the floor!

Mr J.W.HUSSEY, SANDWICH, Kent.	*Civilian - Apprentice D.C.R.E. electrician.*	Incident at Capel-le Ferne u/g hospital.

During the doodlebug period on the S.E. Coast I had, on a number of occasions, to carry out repair works in the underground hospital to the rear of the *Valiant Sailor Inn* at Capel. The hospital had ventilation ducts out to the Warren cliff face, which could be used as emergency exits. On this day, two of us were working in the galleries of beds when a blast of air knocked us off our feet and this was followed by a terrific bang. On recovering from the shock, we made a mad dash to the nearest air vent and discovered that a doodlebug had hit the cliff face just below us. Before long the area below was seen to be swarming with partly stunned rabbits, that were being quickly gathered up by the local troops, as a welcome supplement to their meagre meat ration, by courtesy of Hitler's doodlebug.

Mrs Jean HALL, FOLKESTONE, Kent.	*ATS Clerk - 130 LAA Rgt H.Q., Bouverie Road W, Folkestone.*	Comments on attack, and invasion scare.

I was posted to Folkestone in 1943, staying until 1945, billeted at No. 89 Bouverie Road West; our offices were next door at No. 91. I was a clerical worker and also helped out as a telephonist at the 130 L.A.A. Regiment Headquarters. Later in the year we had to move to more secure premises in Sandgate Road. The battery sites were stationed all around us on the East Cliff, and up at Capel and further inland, and the lads did very well in shooting these deadly weapons down. When I first arrived in Folkestone we had six-foot deep trenches in the back garden which were difficult to get out of when you are only 5' 1'' tall! These were replaced with air raid shelters when the doodlebug raids started.

When that first V-1 came over, we noticed something was dropping behind it and immediately thought that we were being invaded. But this turned out to be a false impression as there was nothing attached to the parachute. We watched many a gun battle over the Channel from the balcony of the Leas Cliff Hall, where the band played louder to deaden the roar of these 'rockets'. We all watched with our mouths wide open, wondering what would happen next after all the shelling we witnessed.

Mrs Phyllis E. BLACKMER,	*A.T.S. Telephonist/*	'Diver' warnings given
Kingsnorth, ASHFORD	*Spotter with 490th*	on A/A site at Hythe
Kent.	*(M) H.A.A Battery.*	and Isle of Sheppey.

I was a member of the A.T.S. and served with the 490th (M) H.A.A. Bty 141 Regiment R.A. as a Spotter/Telephonist and was stationed in Ireland when the Flying Bombs were first launched on Britain. From there some of our gunners were posted to a field, somewhere near Hythe, where we joined them in August 1944. I remember that, although we were under canvas, it was quite pleasant.

On duty the next day, we were told to blow a whistle the instant we saw a flying bomb which, as we had never seen one, was a bit bewildering. However, suddenly someone shouted, "Diver, Diver!" and told us to blow our whistles, which we did. 'Diver' was the name our men gave to these flying bombs, and we got our first sight of one. To me it looked just like a small noisy aeroplane, with flames coming out of its tail.

Of course, by the time that we could see them that closely, they could not be fired on from our gun position. Then, from behind us, we heard the roar of an aircraft and we watched, with baited breath, as the pilot tried to tip the wing of the 'Diver' and send it back to where it had come from. We admired the pilots of these Tempest fighters that came, I think, from Lympne airfield. I recall that, once, a tipped 'Diver' came straight down, fortunately it landed in the field next to us, so no great harm was done there, We did have a fright though, as there was quite an amount of ammunition stacked ready for use.

After a while we were posted to the Isle of Sheppey, still living under canvas, and my memories of that time are mostly - cold, damp mud and barbed wire. It was so wet that we could not wear our boots and gaiters but had to wear Wellington boots. I remember that there was one huge puddle right at the entrance to the Dining Tent. I cannot recall that we actually fired at anything whilst we were there, and on return from leave we went to Green Street Green, near Dartford, where the enemy was the V-2, but that is another story.

Mr J.J.WHYTE, WELWYN GARDEN CITY Herts.	*LAC Gunner 2853 Sqd R.A.F. Regiment at Seabrook and at Hythe Gun Control HQ.*	Incidents at Hythe and a lucky escape near Hawkinge.

The squadron was sent from Lymington, in Hampshire, to Kent, and our camp on the first night after our arrival was on the beach at Hythe. The Bofors Flight was then sent off to Sellindge, and the remainder of the squadron, including the sixteen Hispano Cannons were placed on the cliffs and at Seabrook. We worked a '24 hours on/24 hours off' shift, but not that we noticed any difference. A funny thing happened one night while I was shaving and looking out of a window of the one brick building on our site, housing the toilets and ablutions. The engine of a V-1 suddenly stopped and it started to come down, but then a strange thing happened. The engine re-started and it turned onto its back and headed back across the Channel - somebody would be very surprised when that landed!

At about this time, after I had been taken off the gun crew, I was helping to man the Hythe Gun Control, and had a bicycle to get to and from Seabrook. As I had some time off, I had decided to go for a spin to Canterbury, but as I was going up towards the main Folkestone to Canterbury Road, as it was a bit hilly, I had got off to walk. A man and his son came walking towards me, so they stopped and we had a bit of a chat. The subject was music and instruments, and he told me that they ran a small band locally. After ten or fifteen minutes, I started off again on my journey, but before I had reached the next crossroads, I heard a V-1 explode. If I had not stopped to chat, I would not have been able to tell you this, as it had landed at the point by the road where I would have been, destroying some telephone wires and a farm house.

Mr John COOMBER, FOLKESTONE.	*Civilian - Private in Folkestone Home Guard.*	Comments on V-1s at Folkestone.

It was an exciting time with the V-1's. We would see them perform all sorts of aerobatics over the town, after having been hit by ack-ack and the gyros disturbed, and many that a piloted aircraft could not do, e.g. straight-up, then down in a spiral dive. I saw one performing over Folkestone for five minutes then straighten out and head for London. Another flew between the pier and Sandgate Castle four times, back to the pier after its fourth trip, then off towards London.

We were stationed at a Home Guard post at The Warren and could see the V-1's being launched at night, always in a straight line, on one of three flight paths straight over the pier, the Metropole Hotel or Copt Point. They looked like little red lighted candles right down low over the water, but by the time they reached the coast they were about 100 feet up, just enough to clear the cliffs at The Warren. They would be launched in salvos of seven, so there would be 21 coming over at the time, then Spitfires from Hawkinge (or Mosquitos at night) would go up after them and then again after they had crossed the coast gun belt.

Folkestone-based A.T.S. girls at Bouverie Road West H.G. found their slit trenches were unsuitable. Although provided with surface shelters later, the girls were expected to install them by themselves!
(Photo. Mrs. Jean Jall.)

Major John P. Dimmer Jr
Headquarters Party 125th AAA

"When, in late July 1944 the 125th A.A.A. Battery was informed that it was to go into action against the flying bombs, I was serving as the Battalion Intelligence Officer (S-2). At this time, a friendly British Officer assigned to Brigade Headquarters, extended an invitation to me to watch a 'night shoot' on one of the V-1 'flyways' near Hythe. This British officer's vehicle led the way for my jeep, driven by Private Thompson, to an abandoned house on a road leading to the seafront at Hythe. After darkness had fallen, the officer directed Thompson to a site at the very end of the road; the top of the jeep was taken down and we three stood up in the body awaiting the arrival of the flying bombs. The fantastic show soon began; behind us echoed the boom of the 3.7ins guns, the thumping of the 40mm Bofors, and the staccato rattle of the various types of machine guns, while over our heads curved the multi-coloured tracer rounds.

As the attention of the guns centred on those V-1's which had not been hit over the Channel and were chugging inland, the air in front of and above us, was filled with falling fragments from exploded shell casings, expended machine-gun bullets and even an occasional 20 mm round which was destroying itself after missing a target. After we had passed several exciting hours viewing the battle of the guns versus V-1's my attention was attracted by a rapidly enlarging circle of flame from a V-1, which indicated that the missile was travelling almost directly towards us. As the gunfire against this particular target intensified and the sky in front of us was sprinkled with the flashes of exploding shells, I remarked to my companions, "I hope they don't hit that one!" It seemed that no sooner than I had spoken than the sky in front of us blew up in a gigantic ball of fire; apparently one of the 3.7ins guns had scored a direct hit on the flying bomb. As it was only a few hundred yards away from us, instinctively the British officer and I threw our hands in front of our faces and threw ourselves onto the floor of the jeep.

Much shaken, and with ears ringing, we slowly rose. Having established that neither of us appeared to have been injured, I then noticed that Thompson was not in sight. Fearing that he had been blown from the jeep by the force of the blast, or wounded by flying fragments of metal I called out, "Thompson, are you O.K.?" There was no reply. I looked round the vicinity of the jeep, afraid that I would espy the battered body of Thompson, shouting, "Thompson, where are you?" This cry solicited a response. A bedraggled figure, helmetless, and covered in twigs and leaves, slowly emerged from beneath the hedge at the side of the road. Thompson looked up at us, and in a shaken voice, said, "Captain, if you think I'm gonna stand up in the f.....ing jeep while those f....ing things are blowing up all around us, you're crazy!!"

A 90mm ack-ack gun of 125th AAA Battalion (U.S.A.) well dug in at St. Mary's Bay (golf course), New Romney on 18th August 1944.
(Photo. Kent Messenger via Alan Wright.)

Pilots of 165 Squadron at Lympne enjoy a few minutes respite from escorting bombers pounding the V-1 launch sites in the Pas de Calais. Fl. Off C.H. Lawson managed to 'bag' six V-1's while he was serving with No. 165.
(Photo. S.R. Chambers via Tony Moor.)

The crew of a No. 277 (ASR) Squadron Walrus based at R.A.F. Hawkinge - its distinctive engine note was mistaken for a V-1 in fog when on patrol off Dungeness. Left-right Flt. Lt. 'Drip' Driscoll (pilot), Pilot/Off. Jeff Winfield; WO/AG E.H. Cartwright and Flt. Sgt. Jim Lawrence.
(Photo. Mr. E.H. Cartwright.)

MAIDSTONE, MALLING and HOLLINGBOURNE C.D. DISTRICTS

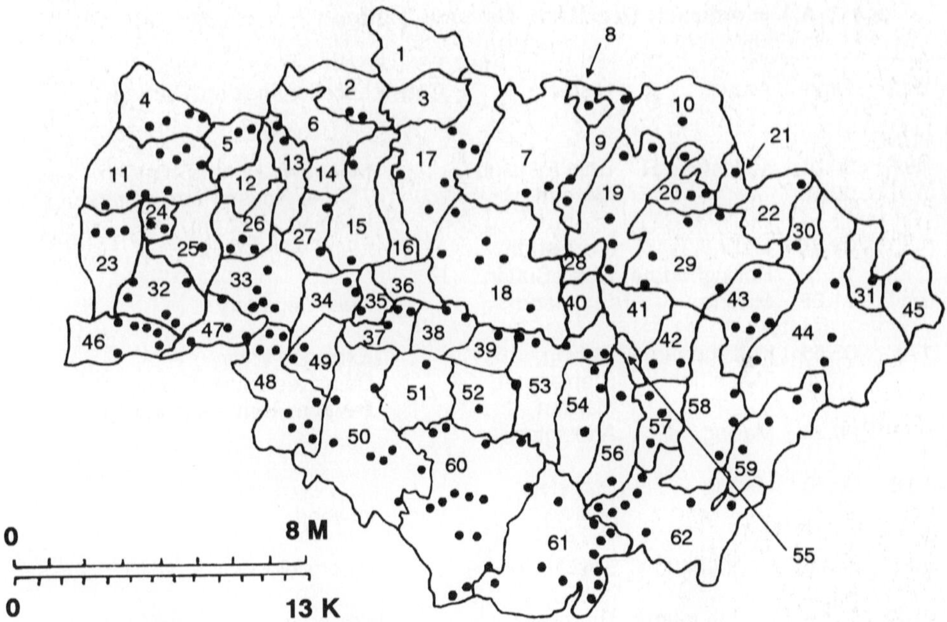

1 WOULDHAM	2 SNODLAND	3 BURHAM
4 STANSTED	5 TROTTISCLIFFE	6 BIRLING
7 BOXLEY	8 BREDHURST	9 DETLING
10 STOCKBURY	11 WROTHAM	12 ADDINGTON
13 RYARSH	14 LEYBOURNE	15 EAST MALLING
16 DITTON	17 AYLESFORD	18 BOROUGH OF MAIDSTONE
19 THURNHAM	20 HUCKING	21 BICKNOR
22 WORMSHILL	23 IGHTHAM	24 BOROUGH GREEN
25 PLATT	26 OFFHAM	27 WEST MALLING
28 BEARSTED	29 HOLLINGBOURNE	30 FRINSTED
31 WICHLING	32 PLAXTOL	33 MEREWORTH
34 WATERINGBURY	35 TESTON	36 BARMING
37 WEST FARLEIGH	38 EAST FARLEIGH	39 LOOSE
40 OTHAM	41 LEEDS	42 BROOMFIELD
43 HARRIETSHAM	44 LENHAM	45 OTTERDEN
46 SHIPBOURNE	47 WEST PECKHAM	48 EAST PECKHAM
49 NETTLESTEAD	50 YALDING	51 HUNTON
52 LINTON	53 BOUGHTON MONCHELSEA	54 CHART SUTTON
55 LANGLEY	56 SUTTON VALENCE	57 EAST SUTTON
58 ULCOMBE	59 BOUGHTON MALHERBE	60 MARDEN
61 STAPLEHURST	62 HEADCORN	

MAIDSTONE BOROUGH and RURAL, MALLING, and HOLLINGBOURNE RURAL C.D DISTRICTS

Key: AA = ack-ack fire BB = Barrage Balloon F = Fighter attack

Date	Time	Area	District	Cause	Location/Incident/Damage
JUNE					
16.6	00.01	Maidstone R	East Farleigh		Meadow - Horse Shoe Inn
	00.53		Marden		Tanner House Farm cottages damaged 1 Sl. Inj.
	04.54	Malling	Mereworth		Map Ref 100713
	10.13	Hollingbourne	Chart Sutton	F	
	11.05	Malling	Snodland		Near Cemetery
17.6	03.55	Hollingbourne	Detling		Exploded in air
	16.00	Maidstone	Staplehurst/ Marden		Damaged caused by cannon fire from Tempest chasing V-1
	20.35	Malling	Addington		
18.6	00.50	Malling	Stansted		
	20.28		Malling		In wood
20.6	23.08	Hollingbourne	East Sutton		Broomfield
21.6	06.12	Hollingbourne	Thurnham		Beaux Aires, between aerodrome and Guildsted
22.6	04.43	Hollingbourne	Bicknor		Admiral Wood
23.6	16.30	Maidstone R	Yalding	F	Near Mill Place 1 K.
	21.15	Malling	East Peckham	F	3 Sl. Inj.
	22.55	Maidstone R	Yalding	F	Shot down and exploded 20 mins later, damage at Laddingford 2 Houses Ser. damaged 25/30 slight damage
25.6	05.30	Maidstone R	Staplehurst	AA	Near Maplehurst
	21.06		Bearsted	F	
	21.50		Marden	F	
27.6	03.55	Hollingbourne	Wormshill	AA	Longwood Farm
	04.37	Maidstone R	Staplehurst	F	
	07.12	Malling	Ightham	F	1 Ser. Inj.
	11.09		Mereworth	F	
	12.10		Detling	F	
	14.07		Marden	F	Damage to farmhouse and cottage, 3 Sl. Inj.

27.6	17.40	Hollingbourne	East Sutton	F	Near Brogden Farm
	18.26		Ightham	F	Damage in Plaxtol
	19.36		Lenham	F	
28.6	13.10	Hollingbourne	Headcorn	F	Leigh Bridge Farm
	18.07	Malling	E. Peckham	F	Goose Green hop garden
	18.10		Plaxtol	F	
	21.20		W. Peckham	F	20 houses badly dam. 1 Ser.Inj.
	22.20	Maidstone R	Staplehurst	AA	Nr gunsite Great Pagehurst Farm. Service casualties - 1 K. 1 Ser. Inj
	22.23	Hollingbourne	Chart Sutton	F	Exploded in air - Amberfield
30.6	09.30	Maidstone R	Marden	F	
	11.15			F	Severe damage to farmhouse
	18.25			F	Hartsfield Farm
JULY					
01.7	10.10	Malling	Wrotham		Exploded in air
	13.10			BB	
	15.24	Maidstone Boro		F	West Beech Drive 200 houses slight Dam1 Ser. Inj. 3 Sl. Inj.
03.7	03.00	Maidstone R	Marden	AA	Nr Military Camp Pattenden Lane. 1 K. 8 Ser. Inj. 8 Sl. Inj.
	22.50			F	Brogden Farm
05.7	00.20	Malling	Wrotham	AA	
	01.48		Mereworth	F	
	06.55		Shipbourne	AA	
	17.57	Hollingbourne	Broomfield	F	
	18.25	Malling	Trottiscliffe	BB	(see Strood/Meopham)
	21.06	Maidstone R	West Farleigh	AA	Kettle Lane
06.7	08.05	Malling	W. Peckham	AA	Oxen Hoath
07.7	15.17	Malling	Birling	F	
	19.10	Maidstone R	Yalding	F	Moors Farm, Collier Street.
	20.40	Hollingbourne	Wichling	F	
	21.07	Malling	Borough Green	F	1 House DEM. 50 Sl. Dam, 2 Ser. Inj.4 Sl. Inj.
08.7	21.56	Malling	Stansted	BB	
	23.15	Hollingbourne			Ramwood Green Farm
	23.16		Headcorn	F	Nr Shenley Farm 9 Sl. Inj
	23.30				Damage to buildings
09.7	00.55	Maidstone R	Staplehurst	F	
	21.50	Hollingbourne	Ulcombe	AA	Nr Knole Hill

10.7	14.45	Hollingbourne	Harrietsham	F	Nr Cherry Garden Farm 1 Sl. Inj.
	19.20	Maidstone B			Exploded in air over cemetery in Sutton Road. 3 Sl Inj.
11.7	09.19	Hollingbourne	Headcorn	F	Borden (Barnden?) Farm
	15.47		Thurnham	F	1 Ser. Inj
	17.49	Malling	Offham		2 Sl. Inj.
	17.50		Plaxtol	F	Damage to Telephone Exchange
13.7	14.45	Malling	Plaxtol	AA	
14.7	18.50	Maidstone R	Marden	F	Chainhurst Dairy Farm
15.7	14.24	Malling	E. Peckham	AA	Minor Damage 1 Sl. Inj.
16.7	00.10	Malling	Wrotham		
	03.30	Maidstone R	Yalding		
	10.20	Malling	Aylesford	F	Bluebell Hill 1 Sl. Inj.
	17.10		Shipbourne		
	17.37	Maidstone R	Staplehurst	F	Exploded in air
	19.40	Malling	Stansted		Hit hill
	23.26		Wrotham	BB	Wrotham Hill Park
18.7	03.40	Maidstone R	Yalding		
	16.29	Malling	Leybourne	F	
	17.37		Staplehurst	F	Exploded in air
	18.12	Hollingbourne	Harrietsham	F	12 houses damaged, 3 Sl. Inj.
	19.40		Stansted		Hit hill
	23.26		Wrotham	BB	Wrotham Hill Park
19.7	01.34	Maidstone R	Yalding	F	Nr Benover
	07.50		Yalding		
	09.14		Marden	F	Chevington (Chevney?) Farm
	10.54		Staplehurst	F	Nr Maplehurst. Farmhouse and buildings damaged.
	11.32		West Farleigh	F	St Mary's Farm, Kettle Lane
	11.55	Hollingbourne	Lenham	F	
	12.15	Maidstone R	Staplehurst	F	Lovehurst Farm
	14.50		Marden	F	In wood 1 Sl. Inj.
	15.25	Hollingbourne	Harrietsham	F	
	23.35		Sutton Valence	AA	
20.7	04.05	Hollingbourne	Boughton Malherbe		
	07.25			F	
	08.20		Boxley	F	

21.7	03.20	Malling	Ryarsh	F	1 Sl. Inj.
	03.25	Hollingbourne	Boxley	F	Nr Sheepwash Damage to 40 houses in Maidstone Boro from this incident.
	06.00	Maidstone R	Nettlestead	F	Nr Vincents Farm
	06.31	Maidstone R	Hunton	F	
	08.30		Staplehurst	F	Gould Farm
	09.30	Malling	Trottiscliffe	F	Ford Place Farm
	18.15		Shipbourne	F	Fairlawne Estate, damage to Ightham Moat
	20.58		Wrotham	F	Damage to Ightham Court and cottages
22.7	16.32	Malling	Ightham	F	Nr Borough Green Road. Damage to Forge House and Ightham Court Ightham Parish Church, P.H and Town House. 3 Sl. Inj.
	23.55		Birling	BB	Leybourne area
23.7	15.38	Malling	Shipbourne	F	
24.7	00.29	Malling	Offham	F	Military Camp, Mereworth Woods
	01.59	Hollingbourne	Broomfield	F	Gravelly Bottom, Kingswood 2 houses badly damaged 1 Ser. Inj 1 Sl. Inj.
	23.13	Maidstone R	Marden	F	Marden Thorn - cottages damaged 1 Sl. Inj.
26.7	02.00	Maidstone R	Marden	F	Damage to property - Marden to Goudhurst Road blocked 1 Ser. Inj
	04.20	Malling	Aylesford	F	Damage to houses 3 Sl. Inj.
	04.22		Otterden	F	Snoad Farm - some damage
	04.30	Hollingbourne	Detling	F	Harpole Farm
	06.40		East Peckham	F	12 Houses damaged 1 Sl. Inj
	07.55		Wateringbury	F	Exploded in air 1 K.
	07.55		Ditton	F	At Research Station
	07.57	Hollingbourne		F	Mantle Farm, Pine Court
27.7	01.17	Hollingbourne	Lenham		Lewsome Farm
	01.42	Malling	Wateringbury	F	
	15.25	Maidstone B		F	Lancet Lane, Loose Road 6 houses severe Dam. 303 houses slight damage 14 Sl Inj.
	16.45	Hollingbourne	Headcorn	F	
	16.50	Maidstone R	Marden		
	17.50	Malling	Wateringbury	F	1 Sl. Inj.

27.7	21.15		Staplehurst	F	1 Sl. Inj.
	22.53	Hollingbourne	Headcorn	F	
	22.55	Malling	West Malling	F	
	23.50		Staplehurst	F	Bletchingley Farm 1 Sl. Inj
28.7	00.15	Malling	East Peckham	F	Exploded in air
	13.40	Hollingbourne	Ulcombe	F	Eastwood Farm
	21.40	Maidstone R	Marden		(Same incident as below?)
	21.43		Staplehurst	F	S. of Marden Road
	22.25	Hollingbourne	Harrietsham	F	
	23.00	Maidstone R	East Farleigh	F	Exploded in air
29.7	19.33	Hollingbourne	Headcorn	F	Nr Barling Green Farm
	21.35		Boxley	F	
30.7	00.57	Maidstone R	East Farleigh		Nr Vicarage
	01.30	Hollingbourne		F	Snarkhurst Wood - exploded in air
31.7	09.54	Maidstone R	Staplehurst	F	Great Pagehurst Farm
	17.45	Hollingbourne	Boughton Malherbe	F	
AUGUST					
02.8	08.30	Maidstone R	Linton	F	Exploded in air
	08.40	Malling	Ightham	BB	
	12.57		Ightham	BB	Boundary House, Town House, Tudor Cottage, Forge House Dam. Superficial damage to church and Ightham Court, 1 Sl. Inj.
03.8	02.50	Malling	East Peckham		Beltring Green Farm 2 Cottages DEM.2 Sl. Inj.
	02.55	Malling	Ditton		Damage to school and church
	03.00		West Peckham		1 house DEM. 1 Sl. Inj.
	03.05		Addington		Addington Park
	03.50	Maidstone B			Exploded in air - Oakwood Park
	04.30	Maidstone R	Yalding	F	The Lees Cottages
	04.50	Malling	Aylesford	F	On railway line
	05.00		Mereworth		
	06.50		Wrotham	BB	West Yaldham Farm, Nr Yaldham Manor
	07.25		Borough Green	BB	Exploded in the air
	08.19	Hollingbourne	Smarden		(Ashford area incident)
	08.56	Hollingbourne	Harrietsham	F	2 Sl. Inj
	09.55		Hollingbourne	F	
	11.50	Maidstone B			On West Station - damage to approx 1180 houses & shops 5 K. 7 Ser. Inj. 40 Sl. Inj.
	11.50	Maidstone R	West Farleigh	F	Nr Ewell Manor

03.8	23.33	Hollingbourne	East Sutton	F	
	23.46		Thurnham	F	
04.8	01.27	Malling	Aylesford	F	
	01.30	Maidstone R	Staplehurst	F	Hushheath Farm, Snoad Wood
	02.27	Malling	Leybourne	F	3 houses damaged & Church 2 Ser. Inj. 6 Sl. Inj.
	03.59	Maidstone B		F	Mays Orchard, Hermitage Lane
	16.25	Hollingbourne	Headcorn	F	N. of Tong Farm 1 Ser. Inj 1 Sl. Inj.
	18.07		Langley	F	Nr Crown & Horseshoe Inn 2 Sl. Inj
	18.15	Maidstone R	Marden	F	Nr Hollidays Farm
	19.45	Malling	East Peckham	F	Exploded in air, over Fountain Inn
	20.10	Maidstone R	Linton	F	Exploded in air, Redwall Lane
05.8	18.58	Malling	Snodland	F	Malling Road - 10 houses Dam. 12 K. 16 Ser. Inj 17 Sl. Inj.
06.8	05.35	Maidstone R	Marden	F	At Chainhurst
	13.30	Malling	Wrotham	BB	West Waltham Farm
	17.10		East Peckham	F	
07.8	06.30	Maidstone R	Boughton Monchelsea	F	Cliffe Cottages DEM. 1K. 3 Sl. Inj.
08.8	01.50	Malling	East Peckham	F	Exploded in air, damage to property 4 Sl. Inj.
	01.52	Hollingbourne	Boxley	F	Entrance to Cobtree Zoo 1 Sl. Inj.
	05.08		Boughton Malherbe		Road from Grafty Green to Boughton Malherbe
	05.35	Maidstone R	Staplehurst	AA	Nr Church, 50 houses uninhabitable 100 Sl. Dam. 2 Ser. Inj. 10 Sl Inj.
	23.15	Malling	Shipbourne	F	
09.8	06.41	Malling	Ightham		4 houses DEM. 20 Ser. damaged 60 Sl. Damaged 2 Killed 7 Ser. Inj. 14 Sl. Inj.
	06.45	Maidstone R	Staplehurst	F	In field at Crump House Farm
10.8	04.30	Malling	Wrotham	BB	Exploded in air
11.8	07.25	Hollingbourne	East Sutton		Chartwell St. nr East Sutton Park 4 Sl. Inj.
	07.29		Boughton		

11.8			Malherbe		Nr Judge House
	23.05	Malling	West Malling	F	
	23.08		Ightham		
12.8	03.07	Maidstone R	Boughton Moncheslea	F	(C.C Type) in the grounds of Boughton Mount 2 houses damaged. 1 Sl. Inj.
	06.20	Malling	Stansted	BB	Exploded in air
13.8	06.14	Malling	Mereworth	F	(C.C Type) In air
	06.22	Hollingbourne	Ulcombe	F	Nr Kingsnorth Manor
	08.00	Maidstone R	Staplehurst	F	Snoad Wood Nr Goudhurst boundary
14.8	06.55	Malling	Aylesford	F	Damage to KA29 factory and 4 houses 4 Sl. Inj
	07.00		Leybourne	F	
15.8	09.00	Hollingbourne	Ulcombe	F	Nr Eastwood House, some damage, 1 Ser. Inj. 1 Sl. Inj
	09.05	Malling	Mereworth	F	On RAF property
	15.45	Maidstone R	Boughton Monchelsea	F	(C.C Type) rear of White Lodge damage to houses 1 Sl. Inj.
16.8	05.30	Hollingbourne	Harrietsham	F	Lower Dene Farm
	05.32	Malling	Birling		
	07.13		Plaxtol	F	Exploded in air. 2 cottages DEM. 4 Sl. Inj
	07.15		Aylesford	F	Some damage to houses 2 Sl. Inj.
	07.15	Hollingbourne	Detling	F	At Detling aerodrome. Damage to flying control and R.C Church. 3 RAF Sl. Inj.
	07.20	Hollingbourne	Headcorn	F	Damage to farm
	09.42		Harrietsham	F	Damage to house & Church in village 1 Sl. Inj.
	16.40	Malling	Snodland	BB	Caused a fire, the balloon cable fell across power lines.
	16.55	Hollingbourne	Headcorn	F	Some damage
	19.55		Sutton Valence	F	Some damage
17.8	06.58	Maidstone R	Linton	F	Rankins Farm
	09.35	Malling	Wrotham	BB	
	13.55	Hollingbourne		F	Greenway Court
	14.50	Malling	Stansted	BB	
	16.29		Aylesford		
18.8	07.05	Hollingbourne	Hucking	F	Court Farm, damage to forge, cottages and Church 1 Sl. Inj.

19.8	03.20	Hollingbourne	Bicknor		Belts Green Farm, some damage
	14.45	Maidstone R	Yalding	F	(C.C.Type) damage to buildings 1 Sl Inj
	21.07	Malling	Stansted	F	Some damage 1 Sl. Inj
	21.09	Maidstone R	Teston	F	Shot down by Meteor fighter
20.8	09.00	Malling	Addington		1 Sl Inj.
21.8	12.55	Malling	Mereworth		Yotes Court
22.8	03.40	Hollingbourne	Thurnham		
	12.30		Lenham		Tophill Farm
23.8	05.34	Maidstone R	Staplehurst		Spilshill Farm - damage to buildings 4 Sl. Inj
	20.46	Hollingbourne	Otterden	F	Well Wood
	20.55		Thurnham	F	
24.8	18.40	Maidstone R	Yalding		Collier Street, Collins orchard 1 Sl. Inj
	19.25	Malling	Wateringbury		Parish Church & Wateringbury Place Military property damaged. 2 Military Sl. Inj.
	19.30		Plaxtol		Damage to 6 cottages and farm buildings 1 Sl. Inj.
25.8	07.15	Hollingbourne	Headcorn	F	
27.8	06.41	Hollingbourne	East Sutton	F	Thornden Farm house damaged
	07.05		Chart Sutton	F	Amberfield Farm
28.8	14.10	Hollingbourne	Frinsted		Madam's Court Farm, cannister of propaganda leaflets found. Lords Hill Cottages damaged 2 Ser Inj. 1 Sl Inj.
	14.10		Headcorn	F	
29.8	12.10	Malling	Offham	F	
	13.36	Hollingbourne	Chart Sutton	F	Slight damage 3 Sl. Inj.
	14.05		Stockbury	F	
	14.05		Hucking	F	(same incident as above?)
	19.22	Malling	East Peckham	F	1 Sl. Inj.
31.8	10.15	Hollingbourne		F	Nr Park Wood Cottages, contained leaflets.

The old timbered-framed Crown Cottages (formerly The Crown Inn) at Staplehurst withstood the blast of an exploding V-1 surprisingly well on 8th August. Peter Hodges, working in his bakery, was only slightly injured when the flying bomb fell in his back yard.
(Photo. S.W. Martin.)

Mr S.W. MARTIN, STAPLEHURST, Kent.	*Building Foreman -* *Emergency Repair Squad,* *at Maidstone.*	Incident at Staplehurst 8.08.44.

I was working for a Maidstone builder, W.T. Burrows, and I had been sent down by Maidstone Rural District Council, who were looking after the bomb damage repairs in this area. I was called out of bed and so didn't see the actual incident which had happened about 5.00 am on the morning of 8th August 1944. The doodlebug actually fell at the top of what is now my back garden. When I arrived in Staplehurst about 6.00am you couldn't get down the road for debris. The remarkable thing was that nobody was hurt, apart from baker Peter Hodges who was working in his bakehouse at the top of the yard next door at the time.

Work had to start, so I rounded up my platoon sent from a camp near Chatham, on Bluebell Hill that housed the conscripted building workers employed on war damage repairs. A lot of them came from Exeter, a crowd from Liverpool and, of course, from the local builders from Maidstone. I think that there were about 200 men in all, and each foreman had his own gang who were sent down by coach each day. During the day the coach driver used to sit and sleep in the yard, as he had to wait to take them back again at night. As far as I can remember the workmen had their own tools as none were supplied, apart from picks and shovels which were sent down - not that they were wanted very often. Usually it was only superficial damage which was caused, apart from at this house and at Mrs Goode's shop across the road. Next door to that, The Firs had collapsed, and Mill House was later demolished, but mainly it was tiles which were blown off roofs by the blast of the explosion. Lime Terrace had all the bricks on the ground floor blown off but the tile hanging above was left intact but it was only single-skin brickwork.

We carried out emergency repairs, covering over the roof with some tarpaulins, and shored up floors, but as this was a timber framed house it had absorbed the blast, as the structure is flexible, but in a brick house it would have been badly damaged, as it is solid. I suppose these repairs took two years in all, including the new windows and re-glazing, but we left the old timbers on the exterior walls exposed rather than re-plastering them. We also undertook repair work to the church, as the tower was damaged and the windows blown out, but while we were working there we found the death watch beetle, so we had to carry out what was necessary to deal with that. I returned to work for a Mr George, who was the local Staplehurst builder, in 1948, eventually moving to Crown Cottages, the property I had repaired after damage, the following year.

Mrs Elva R. MANLEY, SACRAMENTO, California U.S.A.	*Driver - EK District A.T.S HQ Harrietsham.*	Incidents round the Harrietsham area and visiting hospitals.

I was a member of the A.T.S, stationed at their East Kent District H.Q. at Harrietsham. I was a driver, 18-19 years old, and kept a very detailed diary, with perfect notes of the first incoming waves of Buzz Bombs, as our camp was in the small hills overlooking Buzz Bomb Alley. I kept records of damage I saw during my driving duties, as I was the driver for the Chaplain to the Forces at one time, so I went to many sites where V-1's had been brought down by either ack-ack or fighters. I also drove the Commander-in-Chief of the East Kent District A.T.S. and many Ordnance officers.

I also visited hospitals with the casualties, as I drove a large ambulance some of the time and, of course, saw horrendous things. I also saw the lighter side of things. Near our camp was a field with a fallen tree and in the long summer evenings we would sit on this tree and watch the Spitfires chasing the V-1's, either firing on them or tipping them. But I had one terrible experience when I was driving a small utility truck with four soldiers in the back. A V-1 had been tipped and was gliding down in a path at 180 degrees from its original direction. We were almost wiped out by the blast, as it crashed within about 200 feet of us.

Mr George E.ROPER, OTTAWA, Ontario.	*Radar mechanic RCAF at RAF West Malling.*	Incidents with No 85 Squadron, Mosquitos.

I enlisted in the RCAF in Canada and served most of the war in the R.A.F. as a Radar Mechanic on No 85 Sqd at West Malling. The Squadron was based at Swannington when the doodlebug attacks began and returned to West Malling to help intercept them. I was responsible for moving the squadron's Radar Beacon by road; it was mounted on a trailer which was towed behind a Commer lorry. The significant weight of the trailer, and the low power of the lorry, resulted in us having to drive in extra low gear to climb any hill. I recall having to stop often to cool the motor during the final run from London to West Malling. On one such stop we saw the balloon barrage for the first time - most impressive. There was little traffic and the countryside was otherwise peaceful.

I can recall little about the sequence of events, but do remember the high level of activity on the aerodrome, involving extra squadrons, including one Tempest/Typhoon Squadron. We would bet on the outcome of the interceptions, when we were on duty on dispersal for long hours and had a good view of the activities. I suspect that the two doodlebugs which landed near our billets were shot down and exploded upon impact. I recall that it was life as usual in the West Malling area. We continued to visit *The George* and *The Startled Saint* and to go to the dances in Snodland at every opportunity.

Mrs Elizabeth GILLARD, SNODLAND, Kent.	*Resident of Hope Terrace* *High Street, Snodland.*	Incident in Malling Rd, Snodland 5.8.44.

I can remember that it was a Saturday night. We were just having tea, between 5.30 - 6 pm, having just watched the Army lads coming down the road to go for an evening out in Maidstone. Then there was a huge bang. We rushed out, to see all the lads running back to give help - what a fine lot they were! As far as I can remember, three families were killed and one little girl, about 9 years old, who died later in Devonshire Rooms. I doubt if there was a pane of glass left in Malling Road up as far as the Bull corner, and my daughter, who was in the Observer Corps, went up to see the damage. It was dreadful!

Mrs Kate BISHOP, SNODLAND, Kent.	*W.V.S. worker at The* *Devonshire Arms.*	Treating injured at a ARP casualty station.

It was early evening and I was putting my daughter Joan's hair in rags when this thing dropped. I left at once following the explosion, leaving Joan and running to the Devonshire Arms, which was the casualty station. I was in the W.V.S. and knew I might be needed to help.

It wasn't long before the injured started to arrive. I remember it now. Mrs Wallis was dug out alive, and someone told me that at least one man and a woman were killed. Many others were injured. Mrs Hammond and Mrs Piper had hurt their backs. Joan Burlock was thrown out of her window. She was only a girl. The Scouts ran stretcher parties. They were only boys but my goodness they did a great job. My son Peter drove Doctor Mac's car to Wouldham to take one of the injured home, and all evening Mrs Doll Proctor, Mrs Trice and Mrs Nichols made tea at the top school, which is now named 'Homesdale'.

The saddest part of all was the death of little Narcissa Gladdish. My lasting memory of her is of a small, bright child with ginger hair. She was nine years old and had been sent to the top surgery for some medicine for her bed-ridden mother. She must have been close to the explosion when it occurred and had been blown about fifty yards. I can remember her being brought into the Devonshire Rooms. She was terribly injured and died shortly afterwards.

Mr K.W.DRAY, RAMSGATE. Kent.	*R.E.M.E. mechanic with 50th Northumbrian Div.*	6th Guards Tank Regt tragedy near Lenham.

I joined R.E.M.E. upon its formation on 1st October 1942. In 1944 I was posted to the 50th Northumbrian Infantry Division, and I landed in Normandy soon after D-Day. When carrying out a seashore landing it is necessary to hold back the armoured divisions until sufficient land has been captured to enable them to be deployed. One such division held back was the Guards armoured division who were dispersed around S.E. England with the 6th Guards Tank Brigade in mid Kent. Their Field Workshop were deployed at Newlands Stud, near Lenham.

Soon after reveille at 06.00hrs on June 24th, a Flying Bomb, damaged after striking a glancing blow on the local church, crashed into their encampment, causing appalling carnage and damage. Out of a company of approximately two hundred, forty five men were killed outright and of the many who were injured, a further seven died. Our R.E.M.E. base workshop at Ashford came to their assistance in rebuilding the unit ready for movement expected any time, and this same Ashford workshop later sustained considerable damage from near misses by flying bombs, but fortunately with no casualties.

Many of those killed were buried in the R.E.M.E. plot at the Lenham Cemetery. To commemorate the dead the Corps made some new wrought iron gates for the cemetery and badges for the gate pillars. On one pillar is the R.E.M.E. badge (the design was changed after the war) and on the other pillar is the badge of the 6th Guards Tank Brigade. Each year the Corps holds a remembrance service on Armistice Day at Lenham to remember our dead colleagues.

Mr Frank WRIGHT, St JOHN's, Newfoundland Canada.	*Teenager - Maidstone.*	Incidents around Maidstone, techniques of V-1 fighter attacks.

I was born and raised at Maidstone. One cloudy day in early June 1944 I remember hearing a different noise, a deep coughing grunt of a sound. It remained constant; not the sound of an aircraft turning, climbing and evading flak or Allied fighters. A few days later we were told about the V-1. We were chilled to learn that they lacked a crew. They just flew on and on; they could not be scared off by ack-ack fire or a fighter plane. Worse than that deep roar was the sudden horrifying silence when the mechanism cut out. We waited seconds for that mighty crump. Luckily they always seemed to fall on open farms or in orchard country, although those that got through could be seen heading towards London. But before reaching there they had to pass a string of barrage balloons that were strung just north of Wrotham. In fact, on a couple of occasions we saw these balloons 'net' a catch. A flash and the explosion brought the bomb down before it could reach the more populous areas of Greater London.

It was interesting to see how the Allied fighters handled this new menace, approaching them rather like a cat stalking a dangerous mouse or rat, or perhaps a mongoose with a snake. A quick dart to the stern of the bomb, a burst of machine gun or cannon fire, then a very steep bank away from the bomb. Apparently, several Allied planes had hovered too close when firing and were caught by the subsequent debris. On two occasions I saw a very cool approach when a Tempest pilot calmly flew alongside and, with his wing tip tucked under the wing of the V-1, he gently nudged it around. The bomb would head back the way it had come and crash somewhere in the Kent countryside. My brother and his friends who roamed the countryside at that time (it was an ideal time to raid the fruit orchards) were crouching behind a sturdy farm wall, watching a bomb grunt overhead, when suddenly it veered round and came back, necessitating a panicky scaling of the wall to gain the other side for protection.

Mr Laurence B. FIRMOR, MAIDSTONE, Kent.	*Civilian - Farming at Ulcombe Nr Maidstone.*	Incident at Eastwood Farm, Ulcombe 28.7.44.

The bomb that hit Eastwood Farm, Ulcombe, was tipped by a jet and its wing touched a chimney of the farmhouse. It landed in a pile of sawn logs, which scattered about five hundred yards, also about 300 empty apple boxes were blown to pieces and the surrounding orchard had wire, with the remains of the smashed boxes, hanging on branches. Our buildings were badly damaged, even beyond repair, yet luckily no farm animal was badly injured. The horses were in a field joining the farm yard. The only animal to perish was the farm cat, which was found dead in a ditch, and one turkey. A bungalow was shattered by the bomb, all doors blown off - quite a pile up. In one room a basket of eggs were undamaged, yet the roof and chimneys were lifted and the outside walls were badly cracked. People saw the roof and chimneys lift and settle down again. Nobody was in the bungalow; they were in the garden laying flat on the ground.

I was in a strawberry field and the blast just swished through the plants. My wife and mother were in the farmhouse, the roof was shattered, and at first sight we could not expect to see anyone alive, but at times wonders never cease. They were both badly injured. The shock from the experience was very severe; firstly the sound of the missile nearly filled my wife with terror, then her frock was almost ripped off as she fell into a box of thirty-dozen eggs, but she managed to go under the stairs, which saved her from the flying rubble. My mother caught the full blast of the bomb which landed 18 yards from the farm house. Her arms, face and upper body were cut by flying glass, bricks and malt shovels. It was an awful sight; she was found standing up in the debris with only her head showing. No hope appeared to be possible as she was 73 years of age, but she lived another seven years.

Mr Steve BLAKE, MISSION VIEJO, California, U.S.A.	*363rd Fighter Group,* *USAAF based at* *Staplehurst A.L.G.*	Combat Reports of V-1 interceptions.

Capt. James B. Dalglish, 381st Fighter Squadron.

19th June. "I was vectored on to rocket in Hastings area by 'Snackbar' (code name for Controller). When I first saw him, I was at 6,000 feet and the rocket at 1,500 feet. I dove past two Spitfires and a Mustang, which were firing at him, and closed on him indicating about 450 mph. He was indicating 400 mph. Started firing from about 1,000 yards but did not register hits until at about 400 yards. Scored hits at both wing roots and he toppled to the right and went down in a descending turn, finally crashing in a wooded area near Penshurst. This occurred about 2205hrs. Noticed nothing special about the DIVER that I had not read in reports. There was a lot of torque in his slipstream."

25th June, "No friendly fighters present so I went into attack from 5000 feet at 400mph, and got several good bursts in the 'Diver', which made column of flames coming from tail increase. Overshot, but 'Diver' was still on course so I made a second attack which caused the 'Diver' to spin into the ground and explode about 15 miles south of the Thames. Headed south west and picked up another 'Diver' over Headcorn and went into attack from 4000 feet at 350 mph. Got several good bursts into 'Diver', which caused it to loop twice and then hit the ground and explode at about 2320."

1st Lieutenant Russel B. Frevermuth.

27th June. "I sighted a P-plane (pilotless) about 3 miles east of base at about 2005, closed to within 300 yards, chasing it for approximately five minutes, firing intermittent bursts. P-Plane finally swung to right, dove to ground and exploded about five miles west of Maidstone."

1st Lieutenant John Gervan, 381st Fighter Squadron.

29th June. "First seen south east of Folkestone, about mid-Channel, and shot down about 3 to 5 miles from shore, between Folkestone and Dungeness. Altitude 2000 feet; speed approx. 300 mph; time was approx. 2030; range 150 yards. The rocket was below me and I turned into it out of a right turn, closing into range. Fired about four bursts, saw strikes on the machine, bit of the right wing flew off, then the flame stopped and it veered off on its left wing into the Channel."

Pilot group of No. 165 Squadron, scan the skies over Maidstone for Buzz Bombs, waiting their turn to scramble their Spitfire Mk X1. Based at R.A.F. Detling the fighters were only just capable of catching the V-1.
(Photo. via S.R. Chambers.)

The 382nd Fighter Squadron U.S.A.A.F. based at Staplehurst A.L.G. flew North American P-51C Mustangs, and shot down several V-1's. The example here was patriotically named 'Princess Margaret'.
(Photo. Ed Pawink via Steve Blake.)

NEW ROMNEY C.D. AREA

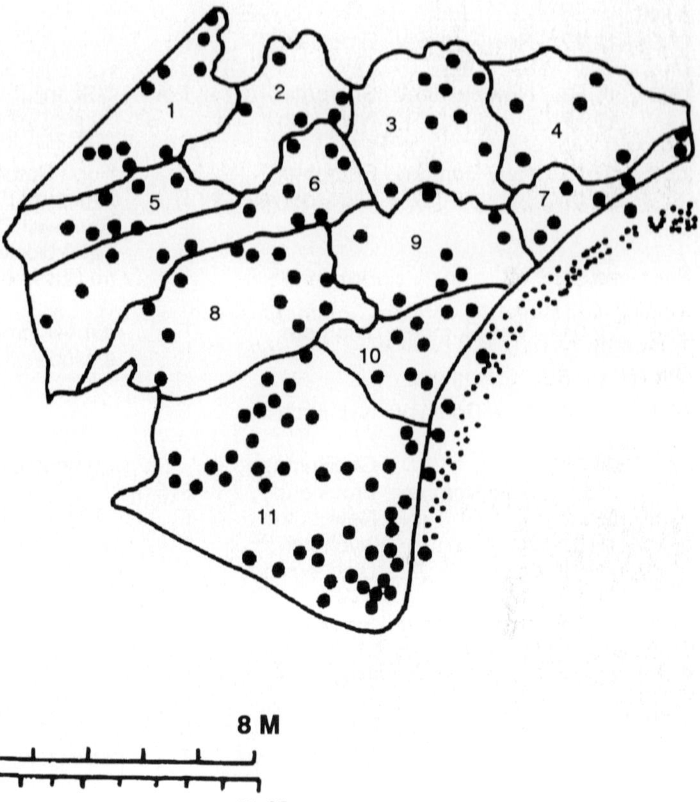

1 SNARGATE	2 BRENZETT	3 NEWCHURCH
4 BURMARSH	5 BROOKLAND	6 IVYCHURCH
7 DYMCHURCH	8 OLD ROMNEY	9 ST. MARY-IN-THE-MARSH
10 NEW ROMNEY	11 LYDD	

NEW ROMNEY C.D DISTRICT

Key AA = ack-ack fire F = Fighter attack

Date	Time	Area	District	Cause	Location/Incident/Damage
JUNE					
16.6	12.20	New Romney	Brookland	F	
18.6	11.53	New Romney	Snargate	F/AA	3 Sl. Inj
	12.47		Ivychurch		
23.6	02.55	New Romney	Snargate	F	Hope Cottage 1 Sl. Inj
	23.01		Old Romney	F	Rheewall Farm, Brenzett on Rheewall Cottage 6 Sl Inj A259 blocked by crater
	23.56		Broomhill		(In Sussex)
25.6	22.04	New Romney	Snargate	F	Almost intact - did not explode
26.6	00.04	New Romney	Ivychurch	F	
27.6	04.30		Old Romney		Crashed
	05.20	New Romney	Brookland	F	
	06.10		Newchurch	F	
	15.50		Ivychurch	F	
	17.05		Old Romney	F	
28.6	06.30	New Romney	Brookland	F	Lambs Farm Kent/Sussex border
	13.00		Ivychurch	F	
30.6	07.35	New Romney	Lydd	F	
	09.42		Old Romney	F	2 bungalows DEM. 2 Sl. Inj.
	09.50		Lydd	F	Exploded in air
	09.50		Lydd	F	Exploded in air (separate incident)
	10.35		Snargate		
	16.30		Newchurch	F	Toll Farm
	16.34			F	Manor Farm
JULY					
01.7	17.30	New Romney	Dymchurch		
	18.50		Burmarsh		
03.7	16.34	New Romney	Burmarsh	F	

04.7	08.15	New Romney	Ivychurch	F	Knowlden Farm
	11.04		Brookland	F	
	14.35		Snargate		Beckett Farm, Fairfield
	21.22		Old Romney	F	
05.7	20.15	New Romney	Burmarsh	F	
	20.40		Lydd	F	Martins Farm
07.7	23.43	New Romney	Old Romney	F	
09.7	21.38	New Romney	Ivychurch	F	
	22.10		Lydd	F	
	22.26		Brookland	F	Hamilton Farm
16.7	16.55	New Romney	Lydd	F	
19.7	12.20	New Romney	Ivychurch	F	
	12.45			AA	
	21.25			F	
20.7	07.20	New Romney	Ivychurch	AA	
21.7	00.01	New Romney	Dymchurch	AA	Exp. in air - St Mary's Road
	00.42		Burmarsh	AA	
	14.45		New Romney	AA	Exploded in air, slight damage to 30 houses
22.7	14.05	New Romney	Lydd	AA	Nr Water Tower
	15.00		Old Romney	F	
	21.25		Snargate	F	Damage to houses in Appledore
23.7	09.12	New Romney	Dymchurch	AA	
24.7	23.12	New Romney	Old Romney	AA	Nr Midley Poor Houses
26.7	01.03	New Romney	St Mary in the Marsh	AA	Exploded in the air
	04.25		Brenzett	AA	
	07.55		Old Romney		On Mil. Camp 1K 2 Ser Inj
	08.00		Burmarsh	AA	Exploded in air
27.7	15.20	New Romney	Lydd	AA	
28.7	13.40	New Romney	St Mary in the Marsh	AA	
	21.32		Burmarsh	AA	
	21.33			AA	
	21.40		Old Romney	AA	

29.7	19.50	New Romney	Lydd	AA	in air - Galloways
	22.57		St Mary in the Marsh	AA	
	23.01		Lydd	AA	Madison Camp 2 Sl. Inj.
30.7	23.53	New Romney		AA	In sea W. of Dungeness
31.7	07.20	New Romney	Snargate	F	
	08.40		Newchurch	F	
	16.37		Old Romney	F	
AUGUST					
02.8	08.23	New Romney	Newchurch	AA	
03.8	00.42	New Romney	Old Romney	AA	
	01.40		Old Romney	AA	
	03.25		Lydd	AA	Exploded in air
	05.30		Brenzett	AA	Snave
	10.45		Brookland	AA	Beans Field
	10.50		Old Romney	AA	Exploded in air. Swamp Farm
	01.45 - 05.40				5 Flying bombs were shot down into the sea by AA fire in the New Romney area.
04.8	01.28	New Romney	Littlestone	AA	
	01.36		Dymchurch	AA	(same incident as above?)
	01.52		Dungeness Point	AA	2 Flying bombs
	02.13		Lydd	AA	
	02.18		St Mary's Bay	AA	
	02.25		Greatstone	AA	
	02.40		Littlestone	AA	
	02.46		Dymchurch	AA	
	03.04		Littlestone	AA	
	03.10		Dungeness Point	AA	
	03.14		Dymchurch	AA	
	04.07		Lydd	AA	
	16.20				Exploded in air
	17.00			AA	In air near Water Tower
	17.25		Dymchurch	AA	In sea
	18.15		Greatstone	AA	In sea
	18.50		Littlestone	AA	In sea
	19.00		Snargate	AA	Lockmill
05.8	04.45	New Romney	Dymchurch		In sea
	04.56				In sea
	07.00			AA	In air over village
06.8	?		New Romney	AA	Coastguard and R.O.C Post damaged
	17.05		Lydd	AA	Pigwell Farm

06.8	03.26 - 05.50				7 Flying bombs were shot down in to the sea by AA fire in the New Romney area
07.8	06.04	New Romney	Brenzett	AA	
	07.18		New Romney	AA	
	10.56		Snargate	AA	Godhall Farm
08.8	05.55	New Romney	Lydd	AA	Nr border with Old Romney
10.8	17.55	New Romney	Dymchurch		In sea
	21.25		Greatstone		In sea
12.8	01.36	New Romney	Greatstone	AA	In sea
	01.43		Dymchurch	AA	In sea
	02.15		Burmarsh	AA	Some damage
	03.02		Dymchurch	AA	In sea
13.8	08.13	New Romney	Lydd	AA	
14.8	04.20	New Romney	Dymchurch	AA	On foreshore
	04.22		New Romney	AA	In sea off St Mary's Bay
	04.22		Greatstone	AA	(same incident as above?)
	06.50		Dymchurch	AA	In sea
15.8	02.00	New Romney	Lydd	AA	Denge Marsh
	04.25	New Romney	St Mary in the Marsh	AA	Haffenden Farm
	08.58		Dymchurch	AA	In sea
	09.04			AA	
	14.04		New Romney	AA	In Sea
	15.40		Dymchurch	AA	Dam to property 4 Ser. Inj.
	17.45		Lydd	AA	
	17.50		New Romney	AA	In sea
	17.55		Snargate	AA	(C.C.Type) Horn (Ham?) Farm
	18.43		Dymchurch	AA	
	18.45		Snargate	F	Godhall Farm
16.8	05.40	New Romney	New Romney	AA	In sea
	07.00		Brenzett	AA	
	18.12		New Romney	AA	Nr Warrens Farm
	18.13		St Mary in the Marsh	AA	
	08.43 - 18.28				7 Flying Bombs shot down into sea by AA off New Romney
17.8	07.40	New Romney	Snargate	F	
	08.25		Lydd	AA	Military - 1 Ser. Inj. 4 Sl. Inj.

17.8	07.15 - 20.44				6 Flying bombs shot down in sea by AA off New Romney
18.8	07.00	New Romney	Ivychurch	AA	
	07.08		Old Romney	AA	Some damage 1 Ser. Inj. 1 Sl. Inj
	06.55 - 07.23				4 Flying bombs shot down in sea by AA off New Romney In addition 17 Flying bombs shot down in sea by AA fire and fighters
19.8	03.13	New Romney	Lydd	AA	Watchhouse field
	03.19		Ivychurch	AA	In sea
	03.26		New Romney	F	In sea
	06.44			AA	In air over Dunes Road
	06.55		Ivychurch	F/AA	exploded in air
	14.35		Brookland	AA	In field
	15.03		Lydd	AA	Lydd Ranges
	21.05		Newchurch	AA	Eammons Farm
	23.30		Lydd	AA	Exploded in air
20.8	06.07	New Romney	New Romney	AA	In sea
	06.18		St Mary in the Marsh	AA	
	07.40		Snargate	F	
	07.45		Lydd	AA	
	11.42		Burmarsh	AA	Farm buildings & R.A.F huts damaged
	14.21		New Romney	AA	In sea
	15.48			AA	
	16.42			AA	In sea
	06.00 (19.8) - 06.00 (20.8)				10 Flying bombs shot down in sea by AA & 1 by fighter off New Romney
21.8	02.15	New Romney	Lydd	AA	Westbrook
	02.18		New Romney	AA	Over sea
	03.59	New Romney	Lydd	AA	In air over Birdskitchen
	04.05		New Romney	AA	Over sea
	13.12		Lydd	AA	Westbrook
	14.30			AA	On shingle North Lade
	19.40		Old Romney	AA	Sycamore House Farm
22.8	03.34 - 04.21				4 Flying bombs reported shot down in sea by AA Fire
23.8	04.44	New Romney	Lydd	AA	
	08.20		Ivychurch	AA	Over sea
	09.05		Lydd		In air

23.8	09.06				In air
	09.06		Ivychurch	AA	Over sea
	09.21			AA	Over Sea
	20.40			AA	In air
	20.43		Lydd	AA	Nr Water Tower
	20.45			AA	In field
	20.49		Burmarsh	AA	Lower Wall Farm
	06.00 (22.8) - 06.00 (23.8)				8 Flying bombs shot down in sea by AA Fire
24.8	02.52	New Romney	Lydd		In air over Denge Marsh
	03.09		Brookland	AA	Old Farm
	06.21		St Mary in the Marsh	AA	Hope Farm
	06.24		Dymchurch	AA	
	06.25		Lydd	AA	In air over Ranges
	07.32		Newchurch	AA	
	02.55 - 06.22				6 Flying bombs shot down in sea by AA Fire off New Romney
25.8	06.38	New Romney	New Romney		In sea
	06.47				In sea
	06.52				
	07.15		Lydd	AA	In air over Denge Marsh
	07.30		Brookland	AA	Lambs Farm
					In addition 2 Flying bombs shot down in the sea off New Romney
27.8	07.20	New Romney	Lydd	AA	Denge Marsh
28.8	14.55		St Mary in the Marsh	AA	Canister of propaganda leaflets found
	15.30		New Romney	AA	In sea
	16.15		Brookland	F	Water House Farm
	17.00		Lydd	AA	
	17.59		New Romney	AA	In sea
	19.20		Lydd	AA	North Lade/Greatstone
	19.30		Newchurch	AA	
	19.40		Old Romney	AA	Newland
29.8	11.20	New Romney	Lydd	AA	1 house DEM. 6 Ser. Dam. 10 Minor Dam.200 Sl. Dam 2 Ser Inj. 9 Sl Inj.
	13.05		Lydd	AA	
	13.15			AA	
	13.50		Greatstone	AA	
	17.00		Brookland	AA	In air Hode Farm
	17.10		Brenzett	AA	Nr Court at Wick Farm

29.8	18.35		Lydd	AA	In air
	20.35			AA	At Caldecott
	12.42 - 23.33				5 Flying bombs shot down in sea by AA Fire off New Romney
30.8	05.00	New Romney	Newchurch	AA	North Fording Farm
31.8	05.46 - 15.52				5 Flying bombs shot down in sea by AA off New Romney

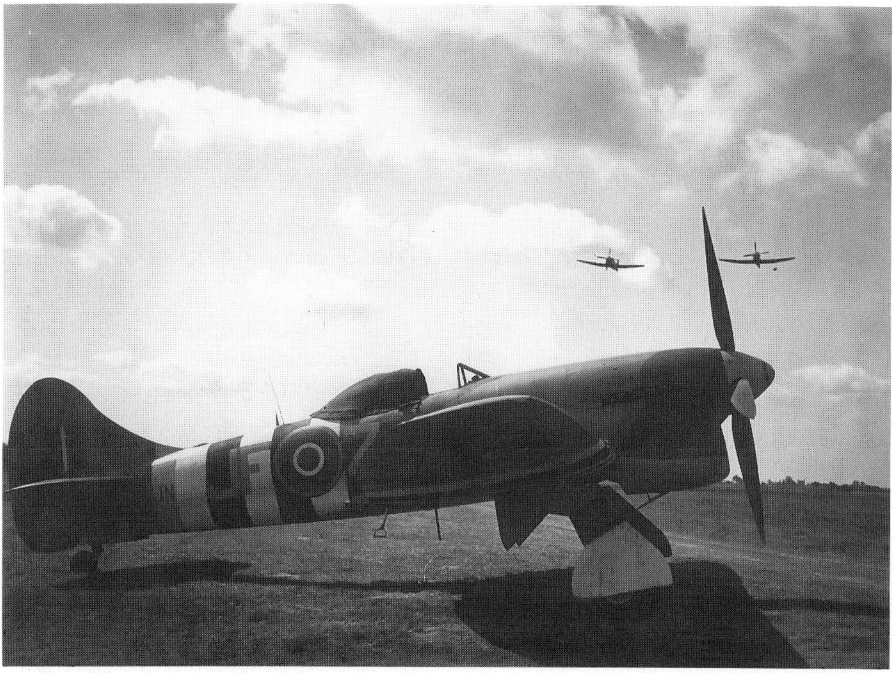

The canopy of this Tempest of 3 Squadron at Newchurch has been covered with canvas to keep the pilot's cockpit cool while awaiting the order for take off. Two colleagues returning from an anti V-1 patrol fly overhead.
(Photo. Imperial War Museum CH14095.)

Mr R.LEVERE, RUGBY, Warks. — *Ground Crew - 150 Tempest Wing, based at Newchurch.* — Incidents at Newchurch and 'Doodle-Bug' Dance.

One day, somebody shouted a warning and pointed to the end of the runway and when I looked I saw a V-1 gliding with a dead engine, looking as if it was going to land on the runway. It was under control but, with no power, it was rapidly losing height. Everybody dashed for what cover they could find. I crashed down beside a petrol bowser, a bit daft when you think of it, and watched the V-1 pass uncomfortably close in its shallow dive until it hit the ground just beyond the airfield boundary. Some sheep that were nearby were the only casualties. Another time was when a Mosquito was coming in to land and when he was almost on the runway threshold, a V-1 passed over the airfield above and just in front of the 'Mossie'. At that moment there were no other aircraft around so several of us, who were on the runway, got a bit excited and waved our arms about and pointed towards the V-1. We never knew if the pilot saw our antics, spotted it himself or received a call on his radio, but we did see his exhaust smoke as he 'piled on his boost', and after a climbing turn, he opened fire at the fast receding V-1. We saw the flashes of the cannon shells while hitting the bomb, which quickly went into a dive and exploded in the open countryside. A remarkable piece of shooting, as the range was then quite considerable and the whole incident probably took place in not much more than a minute or two. Afterwards, the Mossie rejoined the circuit and landed and we all gave the pilot a cheer as he strolled by us. During the month of July a 'Celebration Dance' was organised in Folkestone, to mark the Wing's growing success in shooting down the V-1's. Someone had made a full-sized wood and cardboard model of a flying bomb and it was suspended from the ceiling of the ballroom (The Lees Cliff Hall). During the evening, when several of the lads were amply 'tanked-up' with beer, a human pyramid (or rather a heap of bodies) was formed underneath the suspended V-1 and someone climbed up to the top and grabbed the black-painted monster, bringing it down to the floor. Everyone cheered as the 'flying bomb' was torn to pieces.

P/O S.R.E BARCKLEY, DFC COLWYN BAY, Clwyd.	*Pilot - No 3 Sqd. (Tempest) based at Newchurch A.L.G.*	First V-1 shot down over France?

I was stationed at Newchurch ALG with No.3 (F) Squadron during the V-1 campaign, our squadron having moved there from Bradwell Bay on 28th April 1944, and we remained there until 28th September, when we moved to Matlask in Norfolk preparatory to departing for Grimbergen, Brussels. Whilst at Newchurch, our Tempest Wing (comprising with ourselves No. 486 NZ Squadron and 56 Squadron) provided the main fighter defence against the V-1, shooting down 705 of which 3 Squadron accounted for 305, and I am pleased to say I contributed a number to this score. I believe that I was the first pilot to attack a V-1 in flight. The event occurred on 8th May 1944, on a night intruder operation, when I intercepted a V-1 in the neighbourhood of Evreaux and eventually attacked it west of Le Havre. It crashed into the sea in the area of Deauville. I would point out this was more than one month before the V-1's were launched against England. At the time I was not aware that it was a V-1, and my log book refers to it as a 'JET-SHIP', which showed a degree of prescience on my part. Our period at Newchurch was particularly interesting as it attracted a considerable number of famous people who felt the need to visit us. These ranged from Sir Archibald Sinclair, the Air Minister, and Sir Trafford Leigh Mallory, the A.O.C. and many other famous senior officers. It also brought many film stars, such as Edward G. Robinson and all the famous war correspondents. One, whose fame extended beyond the war, was Ernest Hemmingway, who lived in a tent next to mine, and was the only war correspondent there who got up and down with us, and shared our meagre repast. I had many interesting talks with him, and whilst with us he certainly was not the bombastic hell-raiser of his popular image.

Mr Morian WILLIAMS, Bitterne SOUTHAMPTON.	*Adjutant - No 3 Sqd* *No 150 Tempest Wing* *R.A.F. at Newchurch.*	Experiences while at the Newchurch A.L.G. May - September 1944.

I was posted to Newchurch, Kent, as Adjutant to No. 3(F) Squadron in May 1944, exchanging the luxury of London, in spite of the bombing, for the rigours of Romney Marshes and living in tents. The officer's mess was a marquee, our Wing quarters were bell tents, and the whole of the dispersal area was tented - I did, however, have a converted farm outhouse for an office. At this time the squadron was part of 150 Tempest Wing, with Wing Commander Roland Beaumont DSO, DFC, as the Wing Leader, and had been engaged in sorties over the Channel and preparing for the expected invasion, in addition to attacking the launching sites of the new vengeance weapons of Hitler - the V-1's and V-2's. On Tuesday night, June 13th 1944, the first 'Buzz Bomb' was heard roaring overhead; we rushed out of our tent to see these flaming craft roaring towards London. Rumours were circulating in the small hours. One that control at the end of the runway had given it a green light - thinking it to be an aircraft wanting to land or that parachutists had landed - and we had no ammo for our revolvers! We people on the ground got used to them coming over, sleeping in our tents at night with our tin hats over our faces - and we all anticipated that deadly hush when the motor cut out - and the bomb started circling down, to land who knew where? Our squadron was part of the main force used to attack the V-1's which had penetrated the Channel defences, patrolling aircraft, and A.A. guns along the coast, then the 150 Wing Tempests and finally more aircraft and balloons around London. Most of the time, being summer, was taken up with flying, and opportunities for leave were few, on these occasion a three-ton truck would take personnel to Folkestone for tea dances, films and shopping. Personally I enjoyed my stay at Newchurch in spite of having my 'office' windows blown in. The morale of everyone was high and the friendship has persisted to this day.

Mr Richard S. BODY, ROMNEY MARSH, Kent.	*Farmer - Hope Farm Snargate.*	Effects of V.1 raids on farming community.

First V-1 came in the early hours, and I wondered what it was, that funny sound, then at 8am, later that morning, seeing one, and our local searchlight party firing at it. Anti-aircraft guns were located anywhere, and what went up; came down - cows not liking it, and one ewe was wounded - I think we ate it. We saw aircraft trying to shoot them down, but the Spitfires and Typhoons could not keep up after they had fired one burst of ammunition; but the Tempests and later the experimental Meteors could. Aircraft and guns were operating in the same zone for a start. Anti-aircraft batteries were rushed here from all over the country, and massed along the coast, firing out to sea - so no more shrapnel came inland, and aircraft were not subjected to 'friendly' fire. In fact, the planes took over about three miles from the coast. What a sight it was at night, to see dozens of guns firing one red tracer shell in every five ...... We were told there were some 1500 guns between Hythe and Rye. Once the guns were supplied with Radio Proximity Fuzed shells the kill was probably 90%. When we heard a bomb coming we stopped and watched to check as to it's direction, and when it had passed felt, "That's gone", perhaps a short time later to see a cloud of black smoke, followed even later by a bang. Occasionally, if a bomb had been damaged, it turned round and came back again, and probably crashed. The district was well peppered with bomb craters, but where they landed near a road it was some years before the sub soil settled, and the road had to be continually built up. Most buildings in the Marsh suffered some damage, especially to their ceilings, which were of the old lath and plaster type. Bits of flying bomb were a nuisance in mowers and corn binders, jamming blades.

Mr Derek KENT, SANDOWN I.O.W.	*Bofors gunner - No 24 and 206 LAA Regiments.*	Operation of Bofors guns at Lydd, etc.

I was a Bofors gunner near Lydd during the Buzz Bomb attacks. In common with many other gunners of Light and Heavy Anti-Aircraft Regiments, the gunners from the 24th and 206th L.A.A. Regiments were deployed on the Romney Marshes, near Lydd in the late summer of 1944, against the V-1 attack which had reached its climax at this time. The threat was so great at this time that guns were even brought from the L.A.A. Training Regiments. When we first arrived the doodle bugs approached us nearly head on, but as the Allies advanced and overran the launch sites the later 'Divers' went from right to left, thus giving the 'gun layer for line' quite a job, having to turn on his handles vigorously to keep up with the target. When the target approached us head on, the 'layer on elevation' was able to keep up with it until overhead, then the layer for line would whip the gun round 180 degrees, but as we had guns behind us this did not occur against the 'Divers'. If the Bofors could be loaded quickly enough, it was said it could fire 120 shells a minute. The 40mm ammunition for the Bofors guns was in clips of five, and when they were loaded, a large spring was pulled up to press them down into the breach. As they were fired, the clips were ejected out of a side chute and the empty shell cases were sent down chutes and out the front of the gun. The barrel was interchangeable, so when it got hot (tested by spitting on it), it was changed by four men, using two grips, the rear two having the heavy end, which was screwed into the breach block. The gun was fired by a foot pedal, the order to fire being given when the layer for 'line' and 'elevation' had both shouted, "On Target!" Most of the shells were tracers, which was a great help in getting them on target. But there was a shortage of gunners, and at times there was only the bare amount of four men, whereas the minimum needed on each gun was six or more. On alternate days the gunners had to do 'plotting', i.e. standing in a waist high trench, with a plotting board on the ground in front of them, with earphones connected to H.Q. This plotting board was squared off, and we had to plot the 'Divers' in from one square to another. When a 'Diver' entered the square in which our guns were situated, we had to shout, "Take Post". At the time when the 'Divers' were coming in head on and we hit one, they came down quite close to the guns. We had to take cover in the slit trenches alongside. At this time they introduced the Gloster Meteor jet fighters, and some of our own guns opened fire on them, not having seen or been told of them before. We had a mobile bath unit which came once a week, we also had a mixed battery of men and women with 3.7" guns at the back of our site. At the height of the attacks it just rained shrapnel, sparking on the pebbles as it fell during night attacks. We also had a 'Mad Major' who used to whack us on the back with his stick in delight every time we hit a Diver!

Mr T.A.EVANS,	*L/Seaman - Kite & Balloon*	Seconded to Army
NEWPORT, Gwent.	*Section, Admiralty Pier.*	A.A. at Dymchurch.

I arrived at Dover in January; our berth was on the Admiralty Pier and our C.O. was Lord Graham (Bart.). I was later seconded to the Army and was then stationed in one of the old Martello Towers on the coast at Dymchurch, helping the Army shoot down the doodlebugs as they came over. We used to say to one another how brave the German pilots were, flying through all the gunfire, until we found out there were not any pilots in the doodlebugs at all. The Army gave us some food, but we were hungry for long periods, until a private catering firm helped us out. A few doodlebugs were shot down in the near area but the majority carried on to London and district and did their worst. There were one of two local lads in our group, one being called Buss, a fine lump of a lad, I think from Dover. I volunteered for service in North Western Europe and was shipped to France in July 1944. I was glad to get out of it!

Mr Frank CROWN, MAIDSTONE, Kent.	*Bombardier - Royal Artillery Z rocket battery, New Romney.*	Anti-aircraft guns and 'Z' rockets.

Bombardier Crown F.S. was posted to a 'Z' rocket battery with 32 launchers, sited in a field near New Romney. Each launcher fired two rockets which were about six-feet in length and around four inches in diameter with four tail fins, most had time fuses. The idea was that the launchers, with some slight variation in elevation and bearing, would form a box-barrage of explosions at a certain height, and that a target would be, hopefully, somewhere in the vicinity! Some shells had proximity fuses, with lenses in their noses, which exploded, or were supposed to, on passing a shadow. (I cannot say that this happened.) Rockets were fired electrically by depressing a lever on the side of the projector and, with 64 (sometimes) rockets fired, the brain suffered some disorientation for a few seconds! The drill after firing was to peer over the side of the launcher to check that both rockets had gone; if not, the launcher was swung on a bearing out to sea and left for a period in case of delayed action. Our unit was housed in bell tents near to the rocket site and should a doodlebug land close by, the blast would lift the tents like inflated balloons, and on coming down the pole would pierce the apex and stand erect with the canvass tent draped around its base. In the vicinity were also Bofors and automatic double-barrelled ack-ack guns, all mounted on Pile Mattresses (a brain child of Brigadier General Pile the A.A. Command Chief) consisting of a matrix of railway sleepers and girders, etc. There were also British 3.7ins ack-ack guns, and U.S. 90mm ack-ack guns; so the 'Take Post' order didn't refer to collecting your letters, but to "Get your ear plugs in!"

A group of 'Z' battery rocket launchers which supplemented the anti-aircraft guns on Romney Marsh designed to provide a box-barrage of shrapnel.
(Photo. Imperial War Museum. H6415.)

S.E.LONDON
Districts within old Kent boundaries

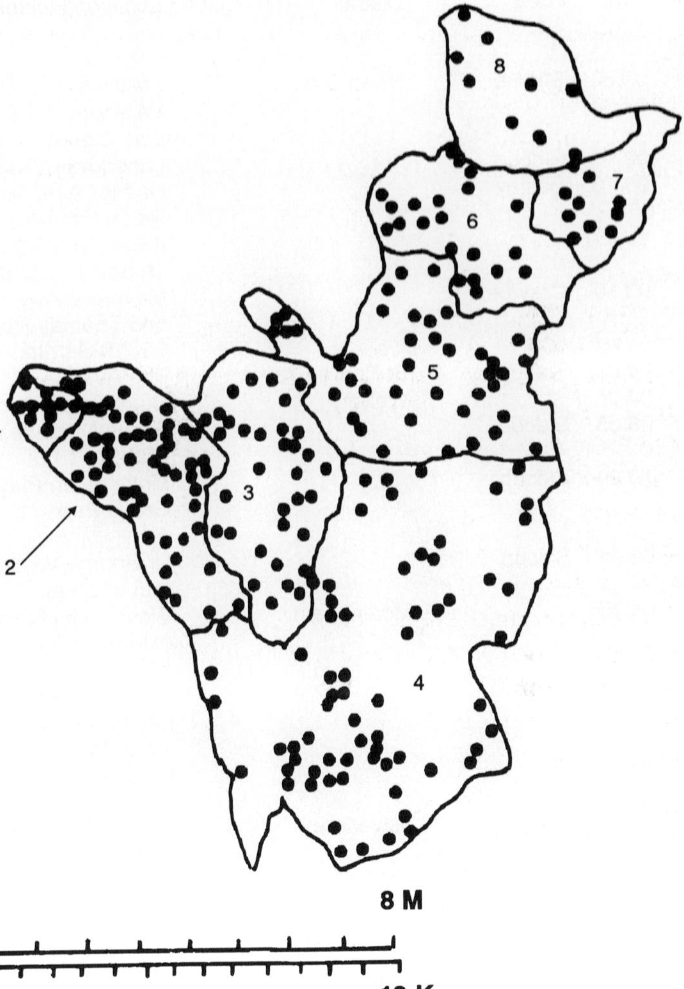

1 PENGE
2 BOROUGH OF BECKENHAM
3 BOROUGH OF BROMLEY
4 ORPINGTON U.D.
5 CHISLEHURST & SIDCUP
6 BOROUGH OF BEXLEY
7 CRAYFORD U.D
8 BOROUGH OF ERITH

SOUTH LONDON DISTRICT 1. (Part of Kent)
BEXLEY, CRAYFORD, ERITH and SIDCUP C.D DISTRICTS

Date	Time	Area	District	Cause	Location/Incident/Damage
JUNE					
16.6	02.30	Sidcup	North Cray		Field west of High Beeches
	02.32				Willersley Park, direct hit on C.D. Depot
	03.00	Sidcup			Lansdowne Road 1 Ser. Inj
	03.10	Bexley			Radnor Ave, Nr swimming pool Rochester Way. 3 houses DEM 6 Ser Dam. 20 Sl Dam. 3K. 19 Ser. Inj. 24 Sl. Inj
	03.10	Crayford			Mayplace Ave, Maiden Lane and Thames Road ext. damage 9 K 19 Ser. Inj. 46 Sl. Inj.
	04.03	Sidcup	St Paul's Cray		The Avenue
	04.35		Welling		Cumberland Ave. (A/A shell?)
	06.55	Sidcup			Evans Nurseries, Priestlands Park Rd 1 K.
	10.29	Sidcup			Mottingham Playing fields, Grove Park
18.6	03.44	Sidcup			Nr Bourne Wood, Hockenden (out of area)
	04.35		Mottingham		West Park/Highcombe Close extensive Dam. 4 K. 6 Ser. Inj 4 Sl. Inj
	04.45	Bexley			Rear of Clinic, Murchison Ave. Extensive damage 2 Ser. Inj. 10 Sl. Inj.
	20.40	Erith		F	In River
19.6	19.50	Erith	Belvedere		In field, Norman Rd 1 Ser.Inj. 2 Sl. Inj.
21.6	05.25	Erith			Southern Outfall, Cross Ness 7 houses Dam. 4 K. 1 Sl. Inj.
	08.00	Bexley			Nursery Avenue - damage 3 Ser. Inj 45 Sl. Inj.
	09.20	Sidcup			Village/ Bunkers Hill 7 Ser. Inj.
	12.35	Erith			Avenue Road/Beechfield Road and Larner Rd. 3 Ser Inj 17 Sl. Inj.

23.6	08.25	Sidcup		Rowley Ave, Blackfen Exten. damage 13 Ser. Inj. 15 Sl. Inj.
	15.05	Sidcup		Old Farm Ave & Crombie Road trapped casualties (Incident taken over by Group 4)
	18.37	Bexley	Welling	Gipsy Rd. 6 Houses DEM. Ext Dam. 10 K.12 Ser. Inj. 44 Sl. Inj
26.6	01.25	Crayford		Between London Road & Bourne Road on open ground 3 Sl. Inj
	02.43	Sidcup		West Park/Highcombe Close 1 Ser. Inj.2 Sl. Inj.
27.6	06.47	Sidcup		Beaverwood Road
28.6	08.50	Bexley		Iris Ave - fell centre of Upton Junior Council School - Ext. Dam 3 Ser. Inj.12 Sl. Inj
29.6	03.15	Crayford	Barnehurst	Trolley Bus Garage, Erith Road 3 Sl. Inj.
	03.19	Bexley		Rear of 58 Porthkerry Ave. 20 houses Ser.Dam. 300/400 Sl Dam. 1 Ser Inj 6 Sl. Inj
30.6	18.05	Crayford		Golf Course, Mayplace Rd. Blast Dam to 240 houses 1 Ser. Inj. 1 Sl. Inj
JULY				
01.7	10.26	Bexley	Welling	Bellgrove Rd, Welling Railway Station Ser.Dam. Extensive blast damage 2 K. 20 Ser.Inj. 59 Sl. Inj.
	12.35	Crayford		Iron Mill Lane, Ext. blast damage 1 Ser.Inj. 6 Sl. Inj
02.7	04.30	Bexley		Bladindon Drive 1 K. 3 Ser. Inj. 7 Sl. Inj
	05.25	Sidcup	St Paul's Cray	SW of Gray's Farm
	05.30	Sidcup		Hockenden Wood
	08.05	Bexley		Upton Rd/Mount Rd - on open ground Riverdale Road 1 K. 2 Ser. Inj 9 Sl. Inj.
	08.51	Sidcup	Chislehurst	Willow Grove 3 K. 4 Ser. Inj 6 Sl. Inj.
	09.10	Crayford	Slade Green	Marshes (Dartford area)
	11.00	Sidcup		In fields off Belmont Lane.
	11.15	Erith	Belvedere	Marshes 400 yds from Abbey Wood gun site.

03.7	01.10	Sidcup		Beedons Field, High Beeches off Neray Road Ext. Damage
	20.50	Erith		Callenders Cable Works, Crabtree Manor Wayand Church Manor Way - fell on air raid shelter 3 Ser. Inj. 20 Sl. Inj.
04.7	18.05	Bexley	Welling	Crocus Road, 52 & 54 First Ave 6 Ser. Inj.22 Sl. Inj.
06.7	03.35	Bexley		Field by Danson Park Lake
07.7	04.35	Sidcup		Old Farm Ave. Ext. Dam, 2 Ser. Inj.2 Sl. Inj.
08.7	23.28	Sidcup	North Cray	Between Mount Mascal & Parsons Lane
09.7	14.40	Bexley	Welling	Unexploded flying bomb, rear of Northumberland Avenue.
	20.35	Sidcup		Berwick Crescent/Days Lane 2 K. 11 Ser. Inj. 26 Sl. Inj.
	20.49	Crayford		Princes Road/Crayford Road 8 houses DEM.12 Ser. Dam 300 Sl. Dam. 6 K. 17 Ser. Inj 15 Sl. Inj.
10.7	10.40	Crayford		Behind Eversley Ave, Venners Farm 300 houses blast dam. 3 Sl. Inj.
11.7	21.00	Sidcup	Mottingham	Clarence Rd. 1 K. 11 Ser. Inj. 20 Sl. Inj.
13.7	15.02	Crayford		Crayford High Street between Crayford Bridge & Bexley Lane 500 houses., 100 shops including Post Office and Civic Restaurant, also dam. 15 K. 35 Ser. Inj. 62 Sl. Inj.
	17.26	Erith	Belvedere	Parsonage Manor Way/Brook St 1 house DEM.1 K. 4 Ser. Inj. 31 Sl. Inj.
	18.06	Sidcup		Ellison Rd. 12 houses DEM. 600 Damaged. 2 K. 49 Ser. Inj. 18 Sl. Inj.
16.7	00.15	Sidcup		Field SE of Cray Valley Hospital,
	00.25	Bexley	Welling	Danson Lane, Danson Rd. damage to St John's Church. 4K. 6 Ser. Inj. 26 Sl. Inj.

17.7	06.33	Crayford		Thames Rd. Tuckers Plywood & Vitbee Flour Mills Dam. 4 Sl. Inj.
18.7	06.13	Bexley		Parkhurst Rd. between Upton Road and Hartford Road. St John's Church damaged again. 3 Ser. Inj. 8 Sl. Inj.
20.7	05.55	Sidcup		Christchurch Rd and Crescent Rd. 2 houses DEM. 1 K. 5 Ser. Inj. 1 Sl. Inj.
	23.28	Sidcup	Chislehurst	Fox Earth, Kennal Rd.
21.7	19.15	Sidcup		Green Lane by Barham Rd. 4 K. 4 Ser. Inj. 29 Sl. Inj.
	19.50	Erith	Abbey Wood	Railway Rd, inside AA Gun Site E end, back of Overton Road. 1 RDF (Radar) set damaged.
	22.32	Sidcup	Chislehurst	Harwood Farm.
22.7	08.00	Sidcup	St Paul's Cray	Chapmans Lane - blast Dam.
26.7	14.27	Crayford		Open ground Nr Mayplace Rd., between Woodside Rd & Manor Rd - 100 houses Sl. Dam. 6 Sl. Inj.
27.7	15.24	Bexley		Gipsy Rd/Sutherland Ave - blast damage1 K. 2 Ser. Inj. 15 Sl. Inj.
	15.36	Sidcup		North Cray Rd 1 Sl. Inj
	15.40	Sidcup	Chislehurst	Crown La. 7 Ser. Inj. 6 Sl. Inj.
	22.54	Sidcup		Field - Carlton Rd. 2 Sl. Inj.
29.7	04.00	Bexley		Open ground S. of Rochester Way Sl. damage 1 Ser. Inj. 3 Sl. Inj.
	14.18	Sidcup	Chislehurst	Willow Grove/High Street extensive damage 5 K. 10 Ser. Inj. 26 Sl. Inj.
	18.53	Bexley	Welling	Hillview drive - 308 Bellgrove Rd. in allotments, ext. blast dam. 18 Ser. Inj. 28 Sl. Inj.
	19.40	Erith		Ramsden Rd - Colyers Lane/Hurst Road.Serious Dam. 25 Ser. Inj 26 Sl. In.
	21.37	Sidcup	St Pauls Cray	St Mary Cray Central School. 1 Ser. Inj. 6 Sl. Inj.

30.7	23.56	Erith	Belvedere	Near Crossness Footpath
31.7	14.59	Erith	Abbey Wood	Field behind Overton Rd. 5 Sl. Inj.
AUGUST				
01.8	07.05	Bexley	Welling	Cleveland Rd. 18 houses DEM & much blast Dam. 1 K 13 Ser. Inj. 24 Sl. Inj.
	15.28	Sidcup		Woods rear of Ruxley Farm
02.8	04.31	Sidcup	Mottingham	Clarence Road, 2 houses & 1 shop DEM. 4 Sl. Inj.
	12.58	Sidcup	Petts Wood	Nr Willett Memorial 1 Sl. Inj.
03.8	04.50	Sidcup		Hartley Crescent - ext. Dam.
	05.00	Bexley	Welling	Allotments Nr Wickham Street
	11.31		Welling	Montrose Ave.
	16.30	Sidcup	Mottingham	London Playing Field, Grove Park Road
05.8	16.46	Sidcup		Priestlands Park Rd, 4 houses DEM 3 K. 2 Ser. Inj. 2 Sl. Inj.
06.8	04.00	Sidcup		Halfway St/Corbylands Rd, 10 shops & Post Office destroyed, ext. blast Dam. 3 K. 1 Ser. Inj. 1 Sl. Inj.
	06.15	Bexley		Bladindon Drive between Penfield Road and Crofton Ave blast Dam 1 Ser Inj. 7 Sl Inj
08.8	01.54	Bexley	Welling	Lansdowne Ave, 6 houses DEM. 2 K. 3 Ser.Inj. 11 Sl. Inj.
	23.05	Sidcup		Maidstone Rd/Upper Ruxley Rd 1 Ser. Inj. 2 Sl. Inj.
	23.14	Crayford	Barnehurst	On Railway line Parkside Ave/ Manor Way 14 Sl. Inj.
10.8	04.14	Sidcup	Chislehurst	Portland Ave/Penshurst - 850 houses Dam.1 Ser. Inj. 11 Sl. Inj.
12.8	01.58	Bexley		Montrose Ave bet. Coniston Ave & Southcroft Ave. 20 houses DEM. 3 Ser. Inj. 19 Sl. Inj.
17.8	20.44	Erith		Bedonwell Rd/Ruxley Rd - 12 houses DEM. many damaged 32 Ser. Inj. 19 Sl. Inj.

20.8	14.10	Sidcup	North Cray	High Beeches 4 Ser. Inj. 1 Sl. Inj
31.8	08.26	Sidcup		Field rear of Food Office, Carlton Road.

On Monday 9th July a flying bomb dived on a house at Welling but failed to explode. The Bomb Disposal Unit later discovered that no detonator had been placed in the fuze pocket - either sabotage or a production line fault.
(Photo. via Bexley Library.)

Mr R. BARROW, BARNSTABLE, Devon.	*Schoolboy - living at St Paul's Cray.*	Incidents at Foots Cray and Orpington.

I lived with my parents at No. 44, Sevenoaks Road, St Paul's Cray, on the main road to Orpington. Our house was about 300 yards from an ack-ack site. One night, after the sirens had sounded, every gun on the camp opened up, the firing was very intense, noticeably so because for a long time there had not been a raid. We heard a loud roar and my mother said,''Jerry is machine gunning the camp.'' I didn't disagree, but the sound was not right. We got up and went to the back door, in time to see what we thought was an aircraft on fire. The flames coming from the rear were too intense to be a plane on fire. Suddenly the noise stopped, the flame went out, and then we heard a swishing sound. After about 30 seconds we felt pressure on our ears, followed by an explosion. The next morning we heard that it was a new secret weapon. A young school friend and myself were told of the wreckage site, so we went hot foot to see it. The doodlebug had landed in some scrubby woodland behind a row of houses, on the right hand of St Paul's Wood Hill, and at the rear of the Grammar School near Crittal's Corner, at Foot's Cray. A still smouldering crater, with some metal work, was being guarded by Police and Home Guard and bits were being picked over and placed in cartons in the back of a vehicle. We were told that this was the first V-1.

I had been home from Hearn's Rise Central School for some weeks with measles, but I was due back on the Monday. On the Saturday, armed with a warden's whistle, I had stationed myself on top of our Anderson shelter to warn of doodlebugs - a Schoolboy Warden! I heard the unmistakable sound of the V-1 approaching, ran in to my mother and told her. My father was in the Army and so Mum was a temporary Refuge Assurance agent, to earn some money to pay the mortgage. She was busy making up her ledger, and said that she would carry on working. Running out into the garden again, I was just in time to see this doodlebug heading right for me. Then its engine cut out and silently it did a complete loop and retraced its route, descending all the time - and crashed on my school. On Monday, on our way to school, we found parts of St Mary Cray were littered with school equipment - exercise books, pens, ink wells and bits of desks - at least half a mile away. On our arrival at school, we were sent home again, so to one that particularly hated school, an extension of absence was most welcome.

Mrs Rosa VAUTIER, DEAL, Kent.	*ATS Sergeant predictor operator on HAA Battery.*	Incidents at St Mary Cray H.A.A site.

During 1944 I was stationed with the 537 (M) HAA Battery R.A. at St. Mary's Cray, Kent, which was an eight 3.7 inch gun site, and I was a Predictor Operator. I can remember the first time that the V-1's were bombing Kent, (the code name we called them was 'Diver'). Our team was on manning duties so when the alarm bells went for action stations on went our steel helmets, and grabbing our respirators, we ran to the Command Post and took our positions on the Predictor, reporting 'Ready for Action', but now we were tracking doodlebugs and not an enemy aircraft, which was a bit different. We were at 'action stations' for quite a while that night, in fact we nearly ran out of ammunition. During a break in the firing we were ordered to 'Stand By' which meant that we could rest but not leave our instruments. I was on the tracker part of the Predictor that night and not very far from our guns. What I shall always remember is seeing a figure in the distance, pushing an old wheelbarrow with a tea urn on it. Our Church Army Canteen manager was coming along to the Command Post, with our Sergeant Cook and two of her girls, loaded with mugs so that we might all have a hot drink. That was one of the best mugs of tea I have ever drunk.

Mr Hal PEARSON, STOCKTON California, U.S.A.	*Member of U.S Signals Detachment at Hall House, Bexley.*	Incidents at Bexley, the Crayford tragedy, and aftermath.

During the last two years of W.W.II, I was fortunate enough to have been stationed at Hall Place, Bexley. We arrived in February 1944 and were there until a few weeks after VE-Day. This posting gave us all in the U.S Signals Detachment a ringside view of Hitler's V-weapons, both 'Buzz Bombs' and the V-2, which he unleashed towards London. Bomb clean-up work details were not an infrequent part of our duty. Hearing and seeing the 'Doodlebugs' and on occasion feeling their senseless wrath and power, we became closer to our civilian friends and allies. One eight hour shift recorded 132 Buzz Bombs that droned over our patch of England. (There's no record of how many cut out!) We had first hand experience with bombings of the Bexleyheath bus garage, the cinema in Sidcup and the resultant damage to Old Farm Road and other surrounding streets, plus many random explosions that would wipe out approximately four houses and damage countless others. Our own personal bomb arrived on a beautiful summer afternoon and, luckily, only blew out all the windows on the street side of Hall Place. All the masonry remained intact, but some decorative lead plates on beam joints in the ancient two-and-a-half storey dining room came crashing down among the on-duty G.I.'s, who were still attached by earphone cords to their radio sets as they crouched for safety under stout wooden tables. What must be the saddest incident of all happened in the parish of Crayford. However, from what we could discern from talking later with the local Air Raid Warden, at that time it was considered that, since the bombings were becoming so frequent and so devastating, evacuation of children was once again to be undertaken. On this particular day, mothers and their children were queued up and were being processed for their journey to safety and security out of the bomb path. It was then that a lone doodlebug came scooting down, in its usual blatantly noisy fashion, and suddenly cut out. The ensuing explosion toppled a wall on to the hapless victims, killing many outright and trapping others, both wounded and dead. The call for troops to help came to Hall Place just as my shift was ending and many of us were on our way in a short time to help in this sorrowful task of recovering victims of Hitler's last contorted gasp.

Mr Peter FINDLEY, MEXBOROUGH, S. Yorkshire.	*Infant survivor of Weald House tragedy.*	Incident at Crockham Hill Nursery School on 30.6.44.

I should state that I was only an infant in 1944 and I lived along with my mother, Kathleen Inwood, at 'Little Mariners' Nursery School at Crockham Hill and then, after its destruction, was moved to the Nursery School where my mother worked - Weald House. My mother was tragically killed at Weald House when a doodlebug was shot down, but went out of control and landed on Weald House. The loss of life on that night, the 30th June 1944, was horrifying; I believe that twenty-one infants were killed, along with eight of the female staff. All those infants were under three years of age, and I have been told that I was one of only three babies to be pulled out of the debris alive. The other account I have been told is that, having had a bout of the measles, I was being taken care of at 'Acremeads', another nursery school some short distance away in Froghole Lane. Unfortunately, after my mother's death, I had no surviving relatives, I was therefore placed in the care of the L.C.C. and had lived at 'Acremeads' for some twelve months after the death of my mother.

SOUTH LONDON DISTRICT 2. (Part of Kent)
BROMLEY and BECKENHAM C.D DISTRICTS

Date	Time	Area	District	Cause	Location/Incident/Damage
JUNE					
16.6	01.25	Bromley			Shearfield Park. 1 K. 4 Ser. Inj 10 Sl. Inj
	03.42	Beckenham			Eden Way 100 houses Dam. 1 K. 1 Ser. Inj. 1 Sl. Inj
	04.00	Bromley			406 Southborough Lane 4 houses DEM. 10 Ser. Dam. 2 Ser. Inj. 10 Sl. Inj.
	04.42	Bromley			Hastings Road, N. of Oakley Road.
	05.45	Beckenham			Tootswood Road, Cottage DEM. 3 casualties
	06.45	Beckenham			Merlin Grove, severe damage, 20 casualties
	08.40	Beckenham			Station Rd/Links Rd, severe damage 2 K. 8 Sl. Inj.
17.6	01.01	Beckenham	West Wickham		Rear of 264 The Avenue 2 houses DEM. 80 Ser. Dam 2 Ser. Inj. 6 Sl. Inj.
	01.25	Beckenham			The Avenue, 30 houses Dam. 1 K. 2 Ser. In.5 Sl. Inj.
18.6	00.35	Bromley			Lakeside Drive, 8 houses Ser. Dam. 45-50 Sl Dam. 4 Ser. Inj. 5 Sl. Inj.
	08.07	Bromley	Bromley Common	F	The Cottage, The Rookery, Bromley Common 1 casualty
	20.35	Bromley			Bickley Park Road, 2 houses Dem. 20 Sev. Dam.
21.6	00.34	Bromley			Mounthurst Road. 3 Ser. Inj. 4 Sl. Inj.
	01.00	Bromley			'Quiet Nook', Croydon Rd 3 Ser. Inj. 3 Sl. Inj
	05.55	Bromley			Princes Plain - School DEM
	09.02	Beckenham			Waste land Bourne Way & Lennard Avenue 1 K. 3 Ser. Inj. 24 Sl. Inj.
	14.10	Beckenham			Hampden Ave/Queens Rd 2 K. 10 Ser. Inj. 46 Sl. Inj.

22.6	07.08 Bromley	Bromley Common	Rosebury Gardens, Cottages Dam. 3 Ser Inj
	11.00 Beckenham		Crampton Road, 6 houses DEM. Whole property between Station Rd/Crampton Rd destroyed 2 K. 8 Ser. Inj. 23 Sl. Inj.
23.6	08.00 Beckenham		Elm Rd/Hayne Rd corner of Westfield Rd.extensive dam. 4 K. 9 Ser. Inj. 21 Sl. Inj
	22.35 Bromley		Open ground Mead Way/Stone Rd 40/50 houses. Ser. Dam. 1 Sl. Inj.
25.6	21.35 Beckenham		The Drive, between Church Avenue/High Street -Severe Dam. 1 K 15 Ser Inj 25 Sl. Inj.
26.6	00.55 Bromley		Young's Garage. London Rd Extensive damage 13 Ser. Inj. 48 Sl. Inj.
	01.00 Beckenham		Queens Rd/Cedars Road 7 Sl. Inj.
	12.45 Bromley		London Rd/Highland Road 5 K. 30 Ser. Inj. 25 Sl. Inj
27.6	03.57 Bromley		Treswell Gardens 3 K. 6 Ser Inj 32 Sl. Inj.
	05.47 Bromley		St Hugh's Sch. partly Dem. 1 Ser. Inj. 3 Sl.Inj.
	08.35 Beckenham		Open ground Nr Rouse Farm
28.6	13.42 Beckenham		Beckenham Place Golf Course
	17.40 Beckenham	West Wickham	The Alders 10 Ser. Inj. 24 Sl. Inj.
	17.41 Beckenham		Rectory Rd 1 K. 2 Ser. Inj. 7 Sl. Inj.
	20.05 Beckenham		Den Road /Shortlands Grove - Shortlands Road.3 houses DEM. 3 K. 1 Ser. Inj. 5 Sl. Inj.
29.6	06.26 Beckenham		Crystal Palace Grounds rear of 69 Crystal Palace Park Rd. 2 Ser. Inj. 13 Sl. Inj.
30.6	01.15 Beckenham		Lennard Rd. 300 houses Dam. 2 Ser. Inj.
	01.26 Bromley		Railway line between Clarence Rd and BromleyStation
	01.38 Beckenham		Allotment Greenview Ave/Altyre Way
	13.40 Beckenham		Churchfields Rd. damage to Railway Bridge - lines blocked 26 Ser. Inj. 29 Sl. Inj.

30.6	15.00 Bromley	Field rear of 'Bonnington House' side of Blackbrook Lane
	20.05 Beckenham	Crystal Palace grounds
JULY		
01.7	11.25 Beckenham	Wickham Court Farm 3 Sl. Inj.
	13.01 Bromley	Martins Rd/Shortlands Ext. damage 20 Ser. Inj. 21 Sl. Inj.
	16.31 Beckenham	Copers Cope Road/Lawn Road 3 houses DEM.1 K. 3 Ser. Inj. 1 Sl. Inj.
02.7	03.10 Beckenham	Albermarle Road, High St and St Georges Rd-Sub Post Office & CD Mortuary DEM. 1 K. 1 Ser Inj 1 Sl Inj
	03.42 Beckenham	Kingshall Road & Aldersmead 2 K. 11 Sl Inj
	04.20 Bromley	17, Lake Ave 1 house DEM. 9 Sl Inj
	07.22	Keston Guest House, Croydon Road 3 Sl. Inj.
	10.57 Beckenham	Golf Course, Beckenham Place Park
03.7	12.57 Bromley	Hayes Common/Baston Manor Road and West Common Road.
	19.05 Beckenham	Allotments Beckenham Lane, blast damage1 Ser. Inj. 4 Sl. Inj
04.7	00.25 Beckenham	Cedars Rd
	22.46 Beckenham	Crystal Palace Grounds
05.7	20.43 Beckenham	Castor Park, blast damage to 100 houses
07.7	13.37 Bromley	200 yds W of Elmstead Station 1 Ser Inj
08.7	21.55 Beckenham	South Norwood Sewage Farm
09.7	21.45 Beckenham	Elmers End Cemetery, Croydon Ave.
10.7	14.21 Beckenham	Langley Park Golf Course. Damage to roof of St. Mary's Church
	19.25 Bromley	Glanville Road/Seward Road 18 houses damaged by blast. 5 K. 37 Ser. Inj. 28 Sl. Inj.

11.7	17.50 Beckenham	West Wickham	High Steet Nr Wheatsheaf Hotel 150 houses Dam.1 K. 11 Ser. Inj 10 Sl. Inj
	17.56 Bromley		In wood SW of Barnet Wood Road.
12.7	09.00 Beckenham	West Wickham	Park Avenue between High St and Woodland Way 12 houses Dam. 400 Sl. Dam 1 K. 10 Ser. Inj. 21 Sl. Inj.
	19.17 Beckenham		Elmers End Rd between Witham Rd and Marlow Rd. 4 shops DEM. 1 K. 6 Ser. Inj. 22 Sl. Inj.
14.7	8.12	Beckenham	Thesiger Road, junction Somerville Road and Old Kent House Rd. 1 K 9 Ser. Inj. 25 Sl. Inj.
15.7	13.55 Bromley		Crown Lane between Victoria Road and Salisbury Road. 3 houses DEM. Many damaged. 1 K. 11 Ser. Inj. 29 Sl. Inj.
16.7	00.12 Beckenham		Copse Ave between Oakland Ave & Boleyn Gardens 300 houses Dam. 1 Ser. Inj. 2 Sl. Inj.
18.7	07.53 Beckenham		Factory Ave, Elmers End, blast damage to Surridges Factory 2 K. 6 Ser Inj 8 Sl. Inj.
	20.33 Beckenham		Elmers End Bus Garage- 9 Green Line Coaches burnt out, garage destroyed by fire. 13 K. 32 Ser. Inj. 28 Sl. Inj.
20.7	06.40 Beckenham		In field, Stone Park Avenue & South Eden Way.1 Sl. inj.
21.7	15.40 Beckenham		Sports ground Nr Copers Cope Road Slight damage to Aerograph, Gallenkamp and Maybury factories. 2 Ser Inj. 1 Sl Inj.
22.7	01.03 Beckenham		Castor Park
	01.05 Beckenham		Aldersmead Road.
	01.07 Beckenham		St Mary's Church, Kingswood Road 5 Sl. Inj.
	02.06 Bromley		Freelands Nurseries, Freelands Road 3 Sl. Inj.
	10.20 Beckenham		Shirley Crescent - blast damage. 4 Sl. Inj.

	13.24	Beckenham		Barnfield Wood Rd - Blast damage 2 K. 1 Ser. Inj. 8 Sl. Inj.
	15.19	Beckenham		Open Ground, Hong Kong Shanghai Bank Sports Ground.
23.7	00.05	Beckenham		Fields S. of Addington Rd. 3 RAF personnel Ser. Inj.
24.7	18.25	Bromley	Keston	20 Lakes Road - 4 houses DEM. 34 Sev Dam 4 K. 28 Ser Inj 6 Sl Inj
26.7	07.25	Beckenham		St James Ave between Westbury Rd & Elmers End Green 1 Ser. Inj. 16 Sl. Inj.
27.7	01.18	Bromley		Ford Ave, 2 Houses DEM. blast damage to many 1 K. 4 Ser. Inj. 2 Sl. Inj.
	01.26	Beckenham		Brameston Rd - blast damage
	15.25	Beckenham	Shortlands	Kingswood Road - blast damage 1 Ser. Inj. 3 Sl. Inj
	15.35	Beckenham		South Eden Park Rd - grounds of Bethlehem Hospital- blast damage 1 Ser. Inj.
	16.45	Beckenham		Ravensbourne Ave - 2 houses DEM 1 Ser. Inj.3 Sl. Inj.
	16.47	Bromley		Shortlands Golf Course 1 Ser Inj
	17.45	Beckenham		Church Rd - blast damage 3 K. 3 Ser. Inj. 6 Sl. Inj.
	21.20	Beckenham		In field Spring Park Woods
28.7	00.02	Bromley		Woodlands Cl.- blast dam 1 Sl. Inj.
29.7	00.25	Bromley		Bexley Lane/Farwell Rd 3 houses DEM 20 Dam.1 Ser Inj. 2 Sl Inj.
	04.00	Bromley		Top of Edgebury 2 houses Ser. Dam. 12 Sl. Dam.1 Sl. Inj.
	13.50	Beckenham		Oakwood Ave/Perth Rd - 3 houses DEM Blast damage to 170 1 K. 3 Ser. Inj. 11 Sl. Inj
	21.45	Beckenham		Wickham Court Farm
AUGUST				
01.8	07.00	Beckenham		Park Court, Laurie Park Rd. 3 K. 4 Ser. Inj. 5 Sl. Inj.
	14.15	Bromley		Wharton Rd 8 houses DEM, blast Dam. 1 K.17 Ser. Inj. 18 Sl. Inj.

02.8	08.18	Beckenham		Bramerton Rd 4 houses DEM, blast many more 4 Ser. Inj 16 Sl. Inj.
	12.55	Bromley		Field E of Pickhurst La. 3 Sl. Inj.
	13.00	Beckenham		Beckenham Rd, 1 Restaurant, 3 Three storey buildings, 7 houses & bakery all DEM. 44 K. 9 Ser. Inj 14 Sl Inj. Kelsey Park, 150 houses Dam. 2 Sl. Inj.
03.8	05.10	Beckenham		Laurie Park Crescent 2 Sl. Inj.
	10.54	Beckenham		Druids Way, off Kingswood Road 7 Ser. Inj 3 Sl. Inj.
	12.20	Beckenham		Abbots Way blast Dam. 1 Ser Inj 8 Sl. Inj.
	12.22	Bromley		Templewood, Sundridge Avenue 2 Sl. Inj.
	12.23	Beckenham	West Wickham	Blakes Recreation Ground
	12.23	Beckenham		Kemerton Rd blast Dam. 2 Ser. Inj.
04.8	16.28	Beckenham		Cherry Tree Walk, 6 houses DEM. blast damage to many more. 1 K. 2 Ser. Inj. 7 Sl. Inj.
05.8	04.41	Bromley	Hayes	Bolds Wood - E of George Lane School.
06.8	13.39	Beckenham		Boundary incident with Group 9 - blast dam. to Bethlehem Hospital Down train to Penge East Station arrived with 5 Ser. Inj. 24 Sl. Inj.
	17.00	Bromley		Wood Drive, Elmstead Lane - blast damage 1 Sl. Inj.
10.8	04.10	Beckenham		Albermarle Rd/Westgate Rd, 2 houses DEM, many damaged
14.8	07.10	Beckenham		West Golf Course, Sundridge Park
16.8	19.10	Beckenham		Grounds of Bethlehem Hospital, Monks Orchard Road
20.8	06.28	Beckenham		Downs Hill between Ravensbourne Ave and Downsbridge Road - 1 house DEM
31.8	17.05	Beckenham		County School Playing Fields, South Eden Park Road.

Mrs N. GOLDSMITH, BROADSTAIRS, Kent.	*WAAF Corporal -* *75 Signals Wing (Radar)* *at Keston.*	Evacuation of unit from Keston to Thanet.

I was a WAAF Corporal in No. 75 Signals Wing (Radar) in 1944 serving at the Headquarters R.A.F. Keston, Nr Bromley, Kent. On Keston Common were many ack-ack (Pom-Pom) guns which shot at the doodlebugs, bursting some in the sky and deflecting others from London so that they came down on the open ground of the Common or thereabouts. Unfortunately, several V-1's eventually hit our unit, damaging the accommodation and finally hitting the Operations Block. We had to be moved and came down to the new North Foreland Radar Station, where we lived in the Convalescent Homes while our new Operations site was established.

Mr Jeff NICHOLLS, MAIDSTONE, Kent.	*Teenager - ATC cadet* *living at Charlton.*	Incidents at Charlton and Blackheath.

It was only a matter of time before the inevitable happened. We'd a long standing arrangement where Ron and I would collect John en route to A.T.C. and all cycle out to Blackheath together. Len made his own way on a different route. It was a summer evening as I headed for John's house, about half way between my house and the A.T.C. headquarters at Vanburgh Castle, Blackheath. I turned out of Charlton Road into Furzefield Road to be confronted by desolation. John's house was about half way along this road with Victorian terrace houses on both sides. Some houses were still standing at each end, but the rest had gone, rubble and debris was piled high and the road impassable. I remember climbing onto the rubble to enquire from the ARP rescue workers, who and where the casualties were but they refused to tell me as it was against the rules. I was upset by this, especially as I was in uniform, so I had to go back to the Warden Post in Charlton Road to ask and eventually I was attended to. The warden's finger ran down a typed list, the worst news was John, his mother and younger brother, had all been recovered dead. His father had survived and was in hospital. It had been arranged that the A.T.C. would participate by parading as a guard of honour on the day of John's funeral, this pleased us as John had been a good friend and was missed by us all. It was a large procession of cars that left St.

John's Church on Blackheath, after the service, making our way to Charlton cemetery for the burial, to lay to rest these three innocent Flying Bomb victims. This was a journey of perhaps three miles or so, and it was arranged that our A.T.C. cadets would dismount from the cars half-a-mile from the cemetery and march the rest of the way. As arranged we formed up behind the three hearses followed by relatives and friends in the remaining cars. We had not marched for more than a few minutes when the sirens sounded, but in any case this sad procession could not in any way disperse, all involved accepted the hopeless situation. It wasn't too long before we could hear a flying bomb approaching; it arrived fast enough that we did not see it; the engine stopped and in seconds the explosion blasted our ears and shook the ground. The mushroom of smoke and dust was on our left, it looked to be about half-a-mile-away. Len, marching by my side, had convinced himself that it had definitely hit his home. His mother would be at home, as this was mid-afternoon on a summer's day. Poor Len had a terrible urge to break ranks and rush home, but somehow he managed to summon up enough restraint to march on with the rest of us. We continued uneasily to the cemetery and eventually were gathered at the grave side, somewhat shaken, and wishing we could be anywhere but there. Where we stood in line, paying our last respects, we had an unrestricted view to the south east. We saw a bomb come over the trees of Castle Woods, at the top of Shooter's Hill a little over a mile away, and heading straight for us, but suddenly it put its nose down and curved to the right to impact in a row of houses on the face of the hill. We silently watched in horror as many houses were reduced to rubble by the explosion, now covered by a lingering pall of dust and smoke, as the grave-side formalities finally drew to a close.

Mr C.R.MUNDAY,	*Student - living in*	Incident in Arngask Rd.
ROCHESTER, Kent.	*Balloch Road, Catford.*	Lewisham 4.8.44.

At this time I was 14, living at 50 Balloch Road, Catford, and a pupil at Shoreditch Technical College and a member of the 5th Lewisham South Scouts at Hither Green Congregational Church, working for my National Service badge involving First Aid, fire-fighting and rescue work. My friend, Len Harford, and myself, sometimes with my father, had taken to cycling to local incidents to help out if we could. On 4th August at about 3.45pm we arrived on the scene of an explosion at the top of Arngask Road; probably within 10 minutes of the incident. This V-1 had landed in the road outside

No 112, and demolishing about seven houses on each side of the road. Several of us climbed over rubble of the odd numbered houses to the back gardens where a lady was standing in a distraught state having come out of her Anderson shelter. She enquired if we had seen a Mrs Kilner in No 111, who usually sheltered under the stairs. We then climbed over the rubble of the partly demolished house but could not get in because of the danger of its collapse. However, the C.D. Rescue Services had arrived by then and several of them worked their way through from the front of the house, but could not find the occupant. As the group stood discussing the next move I suddenly realised that I could see a lady standing close to me, inside a shattered doorway. She was covered in brick dust and merged in with the rubble. She must have been killed instantly by the blast under the stairs, or while making her way there.

Alan & Dorothy FITZSIMMONS, LAGUNA BEACH, California, U.S.A.	*Civilians - living at Bromley.*	Escape from Penge High St. incident.

We were living at the time in Bromley, and saw a great deal of the doodlebugs. First, there was the partial relief when they passed over, but then came the terror when the 'Bug's' engine cut out, and we would frantically dive for protective cover. It was usually some five to ten seconds before we heard the explosion; the damage was always extensive. Our preferred mode of transport, indeed the safest and most reliable mode we had, was the bicycle. On one Sunday, we set out on our bikes, carrying a package, to go down the famous Bromley Hill to Penge. Along the way, the package worked loose, requiring us to stop and re-tie it. Just at that time, a doodlebug came over, shut off and devastated an area of Penge. To our horror, we realised but for our package we would have been in Penge at the time. We were extremely lucky.

Mrs Joan TAYLOR, Grove Park LONDON.	*WAAF - on home leave and visiting fiance's home.*	Incident on Durham Hill, Downham Estate, Lewisham. 4.8.44.

On August 4th 1944, about 1.00pm, a doodlebug fell on No 27 Durham Hill, Downham, killing Mrs Edith Taylor, her married daughters, Mrs Doris Russel and Mrs Vera Hartley, and her little grandchildren Rita and John. Her daughter Vera was home on leave from the WAAF and had just got home having been shopping for a new dress. She was also killed by the blast before she could reach the shelter, together with Mrs Woolfe and her two-year-old son who lived next door. They were all in their shelters and the V-1 landed in their back gardens. I was engaged to Charles Taylor, who was a P.O.W. in Germany; their other son Fred was abroad in the Army. I was serving in the WAAF and arrived home the next day and I went along to Durham Hill in the late afternoon. Their house was opposite St. Barnabas Church (which was damaged together with the vicarage and the church hall) on the corner of Churchdown Road by the clinic. I called not knowing what had happened. I was told that Mr Taylor was at work when the incident occurred. The sad news was passed to Charles by the British Red Cross at his P.O.W. Camp in October. He was repatriated in January 1945, after suffering a nervous breakdown and I married him upon his return.

Mr Geoffrey WICKHAM, CANTERBURY, Kent.	*Schoolboy - living at West Wickham.*	Buzz Bomb Roof Spotter Bromley Grammar School.

June 1944 saw me in my last term at Bromley Country Grammar School in Hayes Lane. As a sergeant in the School Army Cadet unit, I was appointed as an official roof spotter during the Flying Bomb raids. Many pupils and members of staff evacuated to escape the 'Buzz Bombs' as we called them. I remember making my base for roof spotting by the school kitchen (I always was fond of my food) and being given free meals as so many staff who had already paid for the term, had been evacuated in a hurry. It was a traumatic time for all of us as air raid warnings were often sounded after an attack had started, every flying bomb we saw we knew was coming down before it went out of sight. Towards the south we could see what appeared to be every barrage balloon that could be mustered. They had to remain anchored, but if strong winds were blowing, they could be seen bucking like broncos trying to get away. At the end of each day at school, when the kitchen staff went home we usually all left together, but on this particular night one of the well-loved elderly assistant cooks asked if she could go early as she had had a premonition and was a little bit worried about her elderly mother. As she left she said, "Goodbye, everyone," which was rather unusual as she usually said, "Cheerio, see you tomorrow". But we thought nothing of it until she failed to turn up next morning. The cook, who was French, and had the knack of making wartime rations into an exotic banquet, was worried. She told us that normally even if she was going to be late, the assistant cook usually would let her know, but perhaps something had been amiss with her mother. ''After all, she'd had a premonition, hadn't she?'' When the next day she was still not in, and we had had no word, the cook decided that as soon as school dinners were served, she would cycle over and see how she was, as it was only three miles to Hayes where she lived. An hour of so later she returned with the sad news that both mother and daughter had died instantly when their house had received a direct hit from a 'Buzz Bomb', and all that was left of the house was a large hole, filled with rubble.

Mrs Christine RIPIN, NEW YORK, U.S.A.	*Schoolgirl - living in Bexley.*	Incidents in Bexley and at school.

My mother refused to evacuate me to safer areas in the north; my father being in the insurance business was required to stay put and he was also an A.R.P. Warden, so we 'toughed it out'. I was five years old when the V-1 made itself known. My sister was one year old, and one of the first things she learnt to say was, ''doodlebug, Daddy?'' when the ominous drone could be heard in the sky. Sometimes we would be sitting at the table; the drone would be heard approaching, and everyone froze and looked at the ceiling. When the sound eventually faded, my father and mother would relax and continue eating. My days in school were spent constantly on the alert for the whining wail of the Air Raid siren, sitting in a damp shelter with my classmates, being read to or playing 'I Spy' with the teachers; my little gas mask out of its box at the ready. Nights were mostly spent in our Anderson shelter, but sometimes we would be sleeping in the house when the siren started wailing. My mother would grab my sister, a feeding bottle and gas masks; my father would throw me over his shoulder like a sack of potatoes, and down the stairs we'd all dash and down into the damp dark shelter we'd troop, to 'wait it out' by candlelight. We had lucky escapes, thanks to my mother's obstinacy. She refused many invitations to stay at friend's warm, comfortable 'under the stairs' shelters, instead of our cold, damp Anderson and both times the people had a direct hit and were killed. The following morning my Dad would have the grisly task of touring the neighbourhood and helping to dig out bodies where a stray V-1 had dropped on somebody's house.

A welcome sight at any incident was the W.V.S. canteen vans dispensing 'cuppas'. This Mobile Canteen was provided by the City of Scranton, U.S.A. (Photo. Kent Messenger via K.C.C.)

People whose homes were too badly damaged to occupy were often accommodated at local authority 'Rest Centres' such as this one at Beckenham. (Photo. Gilbert Clulow via K.C.C.)

SOUTH LONDON DISTRICT 3. (Part of Kent)
ORPINGTON C.D DISTRICT

Date	Time	Area	District	Cause	Location/Incident/Damage
JUNE					
16.6	03.56	Orpington	Petts Wood		
	05.00		Farnborough		Ninhams Wood
	05.50		Crockenhill		In field E of Crouch Farm
17.6	00.55	Orpington	Cudham		NE of Angus House
	01.02		Biggin Hill		field opposite school Jail Lane
	01.10		Knockholt		N of 'Shelleys'
18.6	09.11	Orpington		AA	Fox and Hounds, Westerham Hill
20.6	20.54	Orpington		F	Warren Rd/Chelsfield Lane, 2 K. 2 Ser Inj. 1 Sl. Inj
23.6	08.50	Orpington	Biggin Hill		On aerodrome, slight damage to Barrage Balloon HQ 2 Sl. Inj.
26.6	01.01	Orpington	Westerham		(see Sevenoaks & Tonbridge)
	01.15	Orpington	Biggin Hill		Pear Tree Cottage DEM. 2 Ser Inj. 6 Sl Inj.
27.6	04.35		Biggin Hill		N. Barrier of aerodrome
	05.25				Ashbourne Rise off Tubbenden Lane,
	18.32				Town Court Crescent, extensive damage 2 Ser. Inj. 35 Sl. Inj
	23.45	Orpington	Cudham		Bombers Lane
28.6	23.00	Orpington	Biggin Hill		Buckhurst Lane
29.6	10.46	Orpington	Biggin Hill		Old Tye Ave. 12 houses Ser. Dam 5 Ser. Inj.9 Sl. Inj.
30.6	03.14	Orpington	Cudham		Fernels Nursery, Spinney Way, Hazelwood Estate.
JULY					
01.7	05.29	Orpington	Biggin Hill		S. side of aerodrome, small shelter hit, 3 believed missing
	10.28		Chelsfield		Skeet Hill (in Sevenoaks area)

02.7	23.34 ?	Orpington	Downe		High Elms Lane. Unexploded, Ccornfield S. of Hang Grove Lane
04.7	10.20	Orpington			N. of Blueberry Farm, Singles Cross
07.7	12.20	Orpington			Field near Eynsford Close 13 Sl. Inj.
	18.25		Downe		North End Lane/Mill Lane. 5 houses Ser Dam. 30 Sl. Dam. 1 K. 3 Sl. Inj.
09.7	21.56	Orpington			Eton Road 12 houses Ser. Dam. 100 Sl. Dam. 14 Ser. Inj 9 Sl. Inj.
10.7	01.43	Orpington	Luxted		Birdhouse Lane
11.7	09.30	Orpington	Knockholt		E. of Rushmore Hill
12.7	15.20 15.37	Orpington	Downe		In air N. of High Street Bushey Viners - some Dam.
13.7	10.08	Orpington	Cudham		Exploded in air - Broomwood
16.7	00.20	Orpington	Downe		Mill Lane, 5 houses Ser. Dam. 30 by blast. 3 Ser. Inj. 5 Sl. Inj
20.7	03.25	Orpington			Cockmannings
21.7	05.35 08.03	Orpington	Crockenhill Luxted		Open ground E. Hall Rd/ Birdhouse Lane 1 Ser. Inj. 1 Sl. Inj.
	10.20		Cudham		Field W. of Angus Home 1 Sl. Inj.
	14.32		Chelsfield	BB	(C.C type) Lillywood
22.7	23.15	Orpington			Berrys Green 4 Sl. Inj.
23.7	01.30 23.35	Orpington	Biggin Hill Chelsfield		Skid Hill Farm Slight damage
26.7	07.56	Orpington	Farnborough		200 yds N. of reservoir
AUGUST					
01.8	06.57	Orpington			NW of Cacketts Farm
02.8	06.34	Orpington	W.Wickham		May's Farm, Layhams

03.8	02.00	Orpington			Field between Singles Cross and Rushmore Hill
03.8	04.00	Orpington	Biggin Hill		Kings Rd. 3 Ser. Inj. 13 Sl. Inj
	05.05		Biggin Hill		on aerodrome
	05.25				Felstead Rd 1 Ser. Inj. 13 Sl. Inj.
	06.00		Downe		High Elms - 13 houses severe. damaged 2 Ser. Inj. 6 Sl. Inj.
	06.50		Downe		Burst in air over village 3 Ser. Inj. 6 Sl. Inj.
04.8	15.45	Orpington	Farnborough		Mill Hill Field
	16.33		Downe		Sow Field.
	19.02		Green Street Green		Warren Rd- 6 houses serious damage 2 Ser. Inj. 1 Sl. Inj.
06.8	04.00	Orpington			Horns Green
	04.05		Farnborough		Field S. of Old Hall
	13.30	Orpington			South Street Farm/Westerham Farm.
	17.10		Knockholt		Burst in air over Station
07.8	23.12	Orpington	Biggin Hill		E. of Westerham Rd - slight dam. 2 Sl. Inj.
13.8	23.00	Orpington			NW of Scots Lodge, Cudham Lane.
15.8	09.08	Orpington			In air over Viewlands Avenue
	14.14		Petts Wood		Wood Ride, 6 houses seriously damaged. 8 Ser. Inj 8 Sl. Inj.
16.8	19.30	Orpington	Knockholt		Park Farm, Rushmore Hill. see also Sevenoaks & Tonbridge
23.8	04.45	Orpington	Chelsfield	BB	20 yds NW of Skeet Hill House
27.8	15.17	Orpington	Green Street Green		Highfield Ave 5 Sl. Inj.
	18.00		Petts Wood		Princes Ave - extensive blast damage. 6 Ser. Inj. 26 Sl. Inj.
	21.15		Biggin Hill		Skid Hill Farm
29.8	17.40	Orpington	Petts Wood		Green Court Rd, 8 houses sev. damaged. 500 Sl. Dam. 9 Ser. Inj. 23 Sl. Inj.

Signals staff of No. 22 Balloon Centre at Biggin Hill, at their telephone exchange - W.A.A.F. Sylvia Slaughter sits on the right.
(Photo. Miss. S. Slaughter via Len Pilkington.)

Constant practice had equipped the Kent Mobile Reserve for the flying bomb campaign. Above: A Civil Defence exercise using their Heavy Rescue vehicles.
(Photo. Kent Messemger via Alan Wright.)

Miss Sylvia SLAUGHTER, READING, Berks.	*WAAF Switchboard Op at No 22 Balloon Centre.*	Incidents at Biggin Hill Balloon H.Q.

I happened to be on duty at the headquarters of No. 904/5 Balloon Squadron, Clapham Common when the signal was received advising that a 'pilotless aircraft' was heading for London. Shortly after this, I was posted to RAF Biggin Hill, where No 22 Balloon Centre had been formed. A tremendous balloon curtain was formed in an attempt to stop the onslaught on the city of London by Hitler's Doodle Bugs. The switchboard was underground, and a long way from the administrative H.Q. and our sleeping quarters. Here I served under Group Captain Drake, Flight Lieutenant Bagnell-Oakley and helped man the telephone switchboard with another WAAF who was named Mabel. She was allowed to 'sleep out' when not required on duty as she was engaged to a civilian called 'Fred' - she used to cycle home to Orpington! The Corporal who was in charge of the switchboard was Gwen Pinchin, from Guernsey.

Mr Maurice REEVE-BLACK, ILFRACOMBE, Devon.	*LAC Fitter/ Armourer at R.A.F. Biggin Hill.*	Incidents at Green Street Green W.E.H.

At the time of the V-1 campaign, I was a L.A.C. Fitter/Armourer in the station armoury at RAF Biggin Hill. I had been injured in a minor accident in an Armadillo (a Ford Armoured car) which was being used to tow a string of bomb trailers. I had been taken to the War Emergency Hospital at Green Street Green. There I was admitted, anaesthetised, the bone was set and I was placed in the recovery ward, a temporary building of wood and asbestos sheet. Because of the constant air raids and warnings, all 'walking wounded' cases were sleeping in an air raid shelter beneath the adjacent railway line. When the air raid sirens sounded during the night, most of the remaining patients were taken there, leaving a few, including myself, who were considered unfit to move. The nursing staff piled pillows around us as some protection should the building be struck. Shortly afterwards, a peculiar engine note was heard coming our way and the increasing sound of anti-aircraft fire, culminated with a loud explosion as the aircraft, so we thought, crashed. Subdued cheers followed immediately by another loud crash as a projectile came though the wall opposite my bed in a shower of asbestos splinters, struck the wall above my head and ricocheted down the ward. The nominal military 'Patient in Charge', an Army staff sergeant, was summoned from the air raid shelter and pronounced that it was a cannon shell, which he moved with an incendiary bomb shovel, to the ground outside. There it was left to be dealt with by a Bomb Disposal Squad. I was allowed to get up in the morning and, having done some bomb disposal work at Biggin Hill (which was still littered with small anti-personnel bombs) I went to look at the 'cannon shell'. I recognised it immediately as a ball round from a 0.50 ins. calibre machine gun and quite harmless. Therefore I took it into the ward to show my fellow patients - to the horror of the staff sergeant. He wanted to know what the b... h...! I thought I was doing. I explained that I was a Fitter/Armourer and well aware of what the projectile was, so he just said, "So why the b.... h... didn't you say so last night?!" and left it at that. During that night we had heard several further dying engine notes, followed by explosions, and realised that something new was in use and this was confirmed on the wireless at breakfast time when Mr. Churchill announced that the Germans were using their new secret weapon. Subsequently a number of other doodlebugs fell very close to the hospital, shattering windows, but the railway embankment alongside saved it from serious damage. I returned to Biggin Hill, but shortly afterwards was posted to a Squadron in India.

Capt. J.L. McCARTHY,	*Cadet at HMS 'Worcester',*	Incidents at Foots
OTTAWA, Canada.	*Nautical Training College.*	Cray Place, Sidcup.

During the period from March 1943 to 1945, I was a cadet at the Thames Nautical Training College, H.M.S. 'Worcester', Foots Cray Place, Sidcup Kent. The cadets and staff had been moved from the ship at Greenhithe for the war period. One evening a party of us heard an aircraft passing overhead, quite low and, as it was dark, noticed flames from the rear of the craft. There was great speculation concerning the aircraft; however, one cadet, an aircraft 'buff', suggested that this could have been an unmanned craft or weapon of some sort. A day or two later the V-1's or doodlebugs started with a vengeance, as many of them crossed Sidcup en route to London. At first we spent some nights in air raid shelters and instruction was disrupted during the day. It was then decided that during the day a sentry would monitor the approach of these V-1's and, if passing on either side, he would take no action, but if seen heading towards the building, he would sound a whistle, at which time all the cadets left their classrooms and went to the basement shelter, for a short period until it had passed. The most notable feature of the V-1 was the distinctive sound of the engine and probably the most disturbing was when the engine stopped. Some of these V-1's glided on, with a distinctive whistling sound, others came straight down. Fortunately, none landed in the immediate vicinity, although I can remember at least one stopping overhead when we were on the sports field, however it glided on. The V-1's were soon regarded as just another aspect of life and were, by and large, disregarded by the cadets.

THE 'ALARM WITHIN THE ALERT' Jeff NICHOLLS

To minimise the lost working hours in industry resulting from air raids, about 1941 a system was devised where all factories appointed industrial spotters who would always be available on the premises during daylight working hours.

The system worked like this, the public air raid sirens would sound. No worker would stop work as the factory would be linked, with many others, by an alarm bell to a local control room. When the action was confirmed by the information filtering down from Observer Corps, Fighter Command, and ack-ack gun sites, via their control rooms, to be a threat to an area the alarm bell would sound in code. The duty spotter and his assistant would leave their work and run to their posts, having first switched the bell to now be received at the post which also contained a telephone and alarm switch.

Assuming the attack was heading your way, the next alarm bell signal would be at a 25 miles radius, followed by another at 15 miles, if coming your way, which was the moment to hit the switch which sounded the factory hooter, putting everybody in the shelter, where they stayed until you received the coded bell signal that the aircraft were now at 15 miles, but going away. You could then sound your 'All Clear' whilst the public 'All Clear' could be perhaps hours later, depending on where the action was happening.

The 'Alarm within the Alert' was designed for bombers with speeds not exceeding 200-250 m.p.h. We had to think quickly when the V-1's arrived at twice this speed. Your first action was to get the workers to the shelters earlier, the second was to man the Spotter's Post full time when the public sirens had sounded, because of the speed of the attack there was never to be enough time to visually locate the flying bombs and decide whether to sound the alarm, or let them pass safely on their pre-set course.

Pte. R. J. Gibbs of the Mobile Platoon 18th London Home Guard (SE) was on duty on the night of 15th/16th June 1944. The following morning he returned home to find it had been destroyed by the first V-1 to fall on London.
(Photo. R.J. Gibbs.)

The L.C.C. Children's Home at Weald House was badly damaged when a V-1 was shot down on 30th June, exploding in close proximity to the building. Some 21 infants and eight female staff were killed, only three infants being rescued alive from the rubble.
(Photo. Kent Messenger via Alan Wright.)

SEVENOAKS, TONBRIDGE and TUNBRIDGE WELLS C.D. AREA

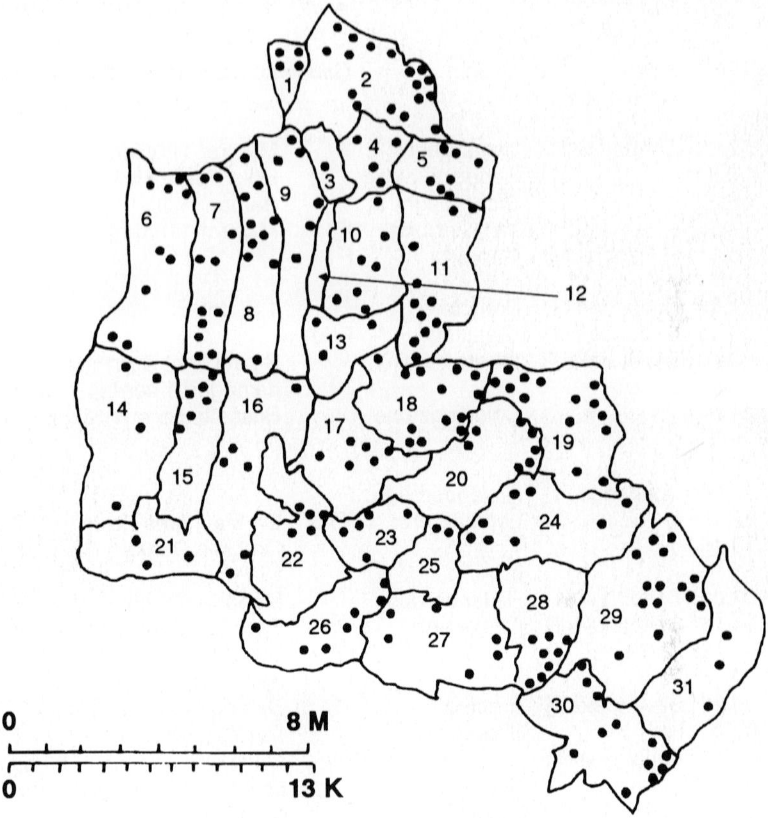

1 HALSTEAD
2 SHOREHAM
3 DUNTON GREEN
4 OTFORD
5 KEMSING
6 WESTERHAM
7 BRASTED
8 SUNDRIDGE
9 CHEVENING
10 SEVENOAKS U.D.
11 SEAL
12 RIVERHEAD
13 SEVENOAKS WEALD
14 EDENBRIDGE
15 HEVER
16 CHIDDINGSTONE
17 LEIGH
18 HILDENBOROUGH
19 HADLOW
20 TONBRIDGE U.D.
21 COWDEN
22 PENSHURST
23 BIDBOROUGH
24 CAPEL
25 SOUTHBOROUGH U.D.
26 SPELDHURST
27 BOROUGH OF TUNBRIDGE WELLS
28 PEMBURY
29 BRENCHLEY
30 LAMBERHURST
31 HORSMONDEN

SEVENOAKS RURAL & URBAN, SOUTHBOROUGH, TONBRIDGE RURAL & URBAN and TUNBRIDGE WELLS BOROUGH

C.D DISTRICTS

Key AA = Ack Ack BB = Barrage Balloon F = Fighter Attack

Date	Time	Area	District	Cause	Location/Incident/Damage
JUNE					
16.6	07.05	Tonbridge R	Lamberhurst	F	Map ref 120/544
	07.30		Paddock Wood		Little Fowle Hall
	08.30		Bidborough		Barden Hall
	11.55		Lamberhurst	F	Map ref 116/543
	14.11	Sevenoaks R	Cowden	F	
17.6	01.58	Tonbridge R	Brenchley		1 Sl. Inj.
	09.05	Sevenoaks R	Sundridge	F/AA	
	20.40	Sevenoaks R	Westerham		Searchlight & Army lorries damaged.1 ser Inj. 1 Sl Inj.
	21.04		Chiddingstone		Bassetts Farm 1 Sl Inj.
18.6	17.50	Tonbridge R	Hildenborough	F	
	22.15		Lamberhurst	F/AA	On Maynards Farm
	23.15				On Little Dunks
19.6	02.08	Tonbridge R	Hildenborough		Meopham Bank
	02.15	Sevenoaks R	Chevening		Back La, Riverhead 5 Sl Inj.
	04.25	Tonbridge U		F	Exploded in air - 200 houses damaged. 1 Sl. Inj.
	08.25	Sevenoaks R	Brasted		Damage to prop. 3 Ser Inj
	09.20		Shoreham		Dunstall Farm
	18.47	Tonbridge U		F	On sports ground - 200 houses damaged 1 K. 2 Ser. Inj.5 Sl. Inj.
	20.37	Tonbridge R	Brenchley/ Paddock Wood		Slight damage 1 Sl. Inj.
	22.05		Speldhurst/ Langton	F/AA	1 house badly Dem 2 Sl Inj
	22.07	Sevenoaks R	Otford		
20.6	05.25	Sevenoaks R	Kemsing		1 Sl. Inj.
	08.30	Tonbridge R	Langton		Holmwood Estate 2 Sl. Inj.
	21.25	Sevenoaks R	Chiddingstone	F	Exploded in the air Walters Green

21.6	00.35	Sevenoaks R	Chevening		Near Irwins Farm
	00.55	Tonbridge R	Speldhurst		Stone Stile, Speldhurst Road
	05.40	Sevenoaks R	Seal		Nr Rumstead Farm, Underriver
	09.45	Tonbridge R	Langton		Chafford Park Farm
22.6	05.08	Southborough			Nightingale Farm
	11.20	Tonbridge R	Lamberhurst	F	Furnace Wood 1 Sl.Inj
	18.34	Southborough		F/AA	Nightingale Farm opposite Moat Farm.Slight damage to buildings 1 Sl. Inj.
	?	Sevenoaks R	Otford	F	Near Vestry Cottage
23.6	04.32	Tonbridge R	Bidborough	AA	
	05.37	Sevenoaks R	Halstead	BB	
	03.15	Sevenoaks R	Chevening	BB	
	06.54		Otford	BB	
	06.55		Brasted	F	Exploded in the air over Quebeque Sq, Westerham
	17.08		Chevening	F	Bayley Hill 2 Sl Inj.
	20.58		Shoreham		Crown Wood 300 yds NE of Oxbourne Fm.
	21.00		Seal		Underriver
	22.37	Tonbridge U		F	Crashed in garden, superficial dam to property 24 Sl. Inj.
24.6	06.25	Sevenoaks R	Shoreham	BB	Preston Hall Farm
25.6	23.30	Sevenoaks R	Shoreham		SW of Clarkes Bottom
26.6	01.01	Sevenoaks R	Westerham		(see Orpington area)
	04.45	Tunbridge W		AA	Damage to farmhouse and buildings 4 cotts Sl Dam
	10.28	Sevenoaks R	Chelsfield		Skeet Hill (in Orpington)
	14.25	Tonbridge R	Hildenborough	AA	
	14.45	Sevenoaks R	Chiddingstone		In River Eden
	16.20	Tonbridge R	Brenchley	F	
27.6	05.35	Sevenoaks R	Cowden		Beechenwood Farm
	06.28		Westerham	F	Squerryes Park Paddock - 100 houses - slight damage. 2 Sl. In.
	07.20	Tonbridge R	Pembury		Dundle Farm
	08.15		Brenchley	F	
	09.22	Sevenoaks R	Hever	F	
	15.19		Seal	F	(in Ightham Parish?)
	16.00	Tonbridge R	Horsmonden	F	UXB? with wings and jet unit complete1 Ser Inj
	18.01		Hadlow	F	
	18.20	Sevenoaks R	Seal	F	(in Ightham Parish?)
	18.26	Tonbridge R	Langton		Exploded in air 9 Sl. Inj.

27.6	20.45		Paddock Wood	F	Lymons Farm
	21.25	Tonbridge U		F	S. Bank of Medway
28.6	07.53	Sevenoaks R	Sevenoaks Weald	F	200yds SE of Beechmount
	13.45	Tonbridge R	Brenchley	F	Longbrooks Farm 2 Sl. Inj.
29.6	01.05	Tonbridge R	Hildenborough	F	
	06.45	Tonbridge R	Hildenborough	AA	Nr Key Point KB2 1 Sl. Inj.
	17.08	Tunbridge W		F	400 buildings slight damage 1 Ser Dam 8 Sl. Inj.
30.6	00.48	Sevenoaks R	Halstead	BB	
	02.35		Kemsing		
	03.37		Westerham	AA	Crockham Hill, Weald House LCC Childrens Home 8 Female staff and 22 children killed. 5 female staff and 4 children Ser Inj. 1 Sl Inj. 1 missing
	11.37		Otford	F	1 K. 6 Ser Inj 4 Sl In
	11.42	Southborough		AA	
JULY					
01.7	02.00	Sevenoaks R	Shoreham		N of Polhill Arms PH
	08.05		Penshurst		Nr Well Place
	10.28		Chelsfield		Skeet Hill (Orpington area)
	10.30		Shoreham	BB	Porters Farm
	12.16		Penshurst		Romney Street Farm
	13.07		Kemsing	BB	Shorne Hill
	16.39		Penshurst		Vexour Farm
02.7	05.50	Sevenoaks R	Shoreham		
	07.30	Tonbridge R	Hadlow	AA	
	08.00	Sevenoaks U			In garden rear of South Park Lodge 2 Ser. Inj. 15 Sl. Inj
o3.7	02.20	Sevenoaks R	Brasted	BB	16 houses damaged
	03.40		Westerham		
	09.10	Tonbridge R	Capel	AA	20/30 houses ser. damage 60/70 slight damage 5 Ser. Inj.
	15.23		Sundridge	BB	Wood at Combe Bank
	16.30	Sevenoaks R	Kemsing	AA	
	17.40		Edenbridge	F	Howlets Farm 1 Sl. Inj
	20.59	Tonbridge U		F	
	21.39	Tonbridge R	Hildenborough	F	near village
04.7	09.10	Tonbridge R	Hildenborough	AA	
	12.26	Sevenoaks R	Sundridge	F	Hill Farm 1 Ser. Inj. 1 Sl. Inj.
	20.35	Tonbridge R	Speldhurst	F	
	21.30	Sevenoaks R	Chiddingstone	F	

04.7	21.48		Shoreham		
	22.00		Sundridge	F	
	?		Edenbridge		Wood on Kent/Surrey border
05.7	00.25	Sevenoaks R	Hever		1 Sl. Inj.
	17.20		Penshurst	F	5 Sl. Inj.
06.7	02.15	Tonbridge R	Pembury	AA	
	04.00			F	
	09.10	Sevenoaks R	Shoreham	BB	Pilots Wood
07.7	01.05	Sevenoaks R	Westerham	AA	Crockham Hill 2 Sl. Inj.
	15.25	Tonbridge R	Capel	F	Brakey Bank Wood
08.7	00.21	Sevenoaks R	Penshurst		Penshurst Place Park
	00.31		Brasted		
	00.58		Hever	AA	1 Sl. Inj.
	23.20	Tonbridge R	Hadlow	F	
	23.28	Sevenoaks R	Westerham		Nr Coakham Farm
09.7	00.32	Sevenoaks R	Brasted	AA	Nr Cliffs Farm
	11.05		Sevenoaks Weald		
	12.05	Tonbridge R	Lamberhurst	F	
	14.15	Sevenoaks R	Chevening	BB	
	14.45	Tonbridge R	Brenchley	F	Goshen Farm, Dam. to bldgs. 1 Sl. Inj
	20.17		Brenchley	F	
10.7	01.30	Southborough		F	111 houses slightly Dam. 1 Ser Inj.
	14.53	Sevenoaks R		F	Exploded in air Bitchet Common
11.7	09.25	Sevenoaks R	Shoreham	BB	Round Hill
	09.27			BB	Round Hill
	13.10		Chiddingstone	F	
	14.40		Sundridge	BB	2 Ser. Inj.
	17.47	Tonbridge R	Hildenborough	F	
	17.48		Pembury	F	Slight Damage to 2 cottages.
	19.20	Sevenoaks R	Shoreham		
12.7	07.22	Sevenoaks R	Brasted	BB	
	08.57		Sevenoaks Weald		Beechmont, military casualties 2 K. 42 Ser. Inj. 2 Sl. Inj.
	16.30	Sevenoaks U		F	Damage to Knowle House
	17.57	Sevenoaks R	Penshurst	F	4 Sl. Inj.
	18.20	Tonbridge R	Pembury	F	
	18.27	Sevenoaks R	Hever	F	
	19.13	Tonbridge U			Barden Rd & High Street, 500 shops and houses Dam. 3 Ser Inj 20 Sl Inj

13.7	10.10	Tonbridge R	Hildenborough	F	(Shipbourne/Malling Rural area)
	15.02	Sevenoaks R	Sundridge	F	Winkhurst Wood
	17.10	Tonbridge R	Lamberhurst	F	
14.7	18.02	Tonbridge R	Capel	F	Stone Castle Farm
15.7	14.25	Tonbridge R	Paddock Wood	AA	
	17.45		Hadlow	F	1 Sl. Inj.
16.7	00.20	Sevenoaks R	Hever		Nr Bough Beech
17.7	04.55	Tonbridge R	Hildenborough		
	07.30	Sevenoaks R	Halstead	BB	
18.7	01.14	Tonbridge U		F	
	06.15	Sevenoaks R	Kemsing	BB	
	17.40	Tunbridge W		F	Damage to farmhouse and 2 cottages 1 Ser. Inj.
19.7	00.15	Tonbridge R	Brenchley	F	
	09.58		Hadlow	F	North Firth Drive
	10.10	Sevenoaks R	Seal		Broomsleigh, Seal Chart
	18.30	Tonbridge R	Lamberhurst		
20.7	06.16	Tonbridge R	Lamberhurst	F	2 cottages DEM. 1 Ser Inj 2 Sl Inj
	08.23	Tonbridge U		F	Trench Wood
	23.15	Tonbridge R	Hadlow	F	Damage to houses 3 Ser. Inj.
	23.31	Sevenoaks R	Dunton Green	BB	Fell in Fort Halstead
21.7	09.07	Sevenoaks R	Sundridge	BB	
	11.15		Shoreham	BB	
	14.06		Brasted		
	20.00	Tonbridge R	Pembury	F	Nr Waterworks
22.7	12.10	Sevenoaks R	Edenbridge	AA	Edenhurst
	19.26	Tonbridge R	Hadlow		
	22.55	Sevenoaks R	Chiddingstone	F	Somerton Farm
23.7	08.25	Sevenoaks R	Brasted	BB	Nr Hogtrough Hill
	15.20		Hever	F	Farmhouse & buildings DEM. 1 Sl Inj
	15.20		Westerham	BB	NW of Court Lodge
24.7	00.20	Tonbridge U		F	In field, damage to Fish Hall farmhouse and buildings
	04.10	Sevenoaks R	Penshurst		4 houses damaged
26.7	04.50	Tonbridge R	Hildenborough	F	
	06.30		Hadlow	F	Goldhill Farm
	06.32	Sevenoaks R	Chiddingstone	F	Sharps Place Farm

26.7	07.55		Sundridge	F	
	14.30	Tonbridge R	Capel	F	Nr church
27.7	01.50	Sevenoaks R	Kemsing	F	Exploded in air
	15.25	Tonbridge R	Horsmonden	F	
	16.46	Sevenoaks R	Sundridge		4 Sl. Inj.
	16.50	Tonbridge R	Capel		Lattice Farm - some damage. 1 K. 1 Ser. Inj. 2 Sl. Inj.
	19.25	Tonbridge U	Frant		Town Court Farm 3 Sl. Inj.
	21.27	Tonbridge R	Capel	F	Quarry Wood
28.7	13.26	Sevenoaks R	Leigh	F	Hale Oak Farm
	13.30	Southborough		F	Unexploded V-1 - made safe by Bomb Disposal Unit RE by 18.50
	22.37	Tonbridge R	Hadlow	F	Exploded in air
	22.40	Lamberhurst		F	Nr Little Scotney - some damage caused in Goudhurst Parish, and windows and door of Finchcocks House
29.7	19.35	Sevenoaks R	Sundridge	BB	Shoot Field
	21.40	Tonbridge R	Hadlow	F	1 Sl. Inj
	21.45		Brenchley	F	(fell at Matfield, E.Sussex)
30.7	18.15	Sevenoaks R	Edenbridge	F	
31.7	15.00	Tonbridge R	Pembury	F	1 Sl. Inj.
	15.01	Sevenoaks R	Chevening	BB	
	15.25		Westerham		Nr Betsoms Farm
AUGUST					
01.8	14.13	Sevenoaks R	Seal		2 houses damaged 1 Sl. Inj.
	14.15		Dunton Green	BB	
02.8	04.15	Sevenoaks R	Leigh		Stidolphs (?) Farm
	06.22		Seal	BB	Underriver
03.8	02.15	Tunbridge U		AA	Damage to North Sewage Farm buildings and 10 cottages
	02.57	Sevenoaks R	Penshurst		Elliotts Farm
	03.10	Tonbridge R	Capel		Prowles Gill Farm
	03.15		Capel		Postern Park Farm (same incident?)
	06.04	Sevenoaks R	Seal	BB	Nr Underriver
	08.20		Edenbridge		1 Sl. Inj
	01.25		Brasted		Silverstead Lane
	09.18		Sundridge	BB	In field
	09.51		Seal	F	Underriver
	12.15	Tonbridge R	Lamberhurst	F	
	?		Bidborough		

04.8	02.30	Tonbridge R	Hadlow	F	
	03.48	Sevenoaks R	Kemsing		1 house Dem. 2 Sl. Inj.
	16.25	Tonbridge R	Hadlow	F	Nr Dane Park Farm
	19.00		Speldhurst	F	Shadwell Wood (Tunbridge Wells area)
	19.35		Lamberhurst	F	
	20.23		Bidborough	F	Exploded in air
	20.25	Sevenoaks R	Leigh	F	In hopfield
05.8	04.43	Tonbridge R	Brenchley		Damage to farm at Matfield, E. Sussex
	06.55		Hadlow	F	Damage to cottages
	07.10		Brenchley	F	Damage to cottages
	07.10	Sevenoaks R	Sevenoaks Weald	BB	
06.8	03.33	Sevenoaks R	Chevening		Green Lane Wood
	04.53		Westerham	BB	
	05.55	Tonbridge R	Brenchley	F	
	13.27	Sevenoaks R	Shoreham	BB	Sepham Farm
	13.30		Sundridge	BB	Nr Emmetts House
	13.45	Tonbridge R	Bidborough	F	In air
	17.05	Tunbridge W			On Common, 244 houses slightly damaged 1 K. 4 Sl. Inj.
	17.05				S. of Blackhurst House, Pembury Road 51 houses Sl Dam. 4 Sl. Inj
	17.10	Sevenoaks R	Halstead	BB	In air
	23.12		Brasted		1 Sl. Inj.
07.8	06.30	Sevenoaks R	Cowden	F	
08.8	01.47	Sevenoaks R	Kemsing		N of St Clere
	05.10	Tonbridge R	Horsmonden	F	
	08.57		Bidborough	F	In air - report confirms that this Flying Bomb was carrying at least 24 1-kilo incendiary bombs *
09.8	06.40	Tonbridge R	Lamberhurst	F	12 incendiary bombs exploded causing slight damage *
	06.47	Sevenoaks R	Shoreham	BB	Combe Hollow
11.8	23.10		Kemsing	BB	2 Ser. Inj 2 Sl. Inj
	23.16	Sevenoaks R	Shoreham	BB	2 Sl. Inj.
12.8	01.23	Tonbridge R	Hadlow	F	
13.8	04.00	Sevenoaks R	Seal		8 houses slight Dam.
14.8	00.50	Sevenoaks R	Leigh	F	Slight damage to farm buildings

15.8	09.05	Sevenoaks R	Brasted	BB	Nr Wierdale Manor
	14.10	Tonbridge R	Speldhurst	F	Exploded in air
16.8	17.45	Tonbridge R	Hadlow	F	Damage to Oast House & Cottage
	19.07		Speldhurst	F	
	19.10		Horsmonden	F	Damage to farm buildings 1 Sl. Inj.
	19.50	Sevenoaks R	Chevening	BB	Balloon cables across Knockholt Road incident in Orpington area
19.8	03.17	Sevenoaks R	Brasted		Brook Farm, Toys Hill
	14.35		Dunton Green	BB	Sepham Farm
	23.25	Tonbridge R	Capel	F	Castle Hill Wood
20.8	06.40	Tonbridge R	Speldhurst	F	In air 2 Sl. Inj.
	08.55	Tonbridge U		F	In air over Fishall Farm,
	11.00	Tonbridge R	Brenchley		
	12.27	Tunbridge U		F	On S. Rly, damage between Tonbridge and Leigh, damage to Haversdown House
21.8	02.30	Tonbridge R	Paddock Wood		Durrants Farm
	11.25	Sevenoaks R	Shoreham	BB	In air Filston Farm
	12.24		Leigh		Tonbridge/Redhill Rly. line blocked
	12.25		Seal	BB	Nr Carters Hill, Underriver
	14.40		Sundridge		Ide Hill
22.8	04.10	Sevenoaks R	Seal		
	07.50		Seal	BB	Penfield Farm
	?		Shoreham		
23.8	07.10	Tonbridge R	Brenchley	F	In air Nr Beston Farm
	20.55		Brenchley	F	(C.C.Type) slight damage
27.8	06.45	Tonbridge R	Brenchley	F	Damage to property 2 Sl. Inj.
29.8	11.20	Sevenoaks U		BB	In Knole Road, blast damage to many houses 13 Ser. Inj. 4 Sl. Inj.
	13.01	Sevenoaks U			2 houses damaged 6 Sl. Inj.
	13.14	Sevenoaks R	Otford	BB	2 houses DEM. 6 badly damaged Pilgrims Way. 2 K. 1 Ser Inj.
	14.00		Leigh	F	Contained leaflets
	14.40		Sevenoaks Weald	F	
	18.45	Tonbridge R	Hildenborough	F/BB	
	20.18	Sevenoaks U			Ashgrove Road, damage by blast to West Heath & Shaftsbury House. 11 Sl. Inj.

Despite warnings from R.A.F. Controllers and warning rockets fired by R.O.C. personnel, tragically some fighter pilots followed the flying bombs too close to the steel cables - and paid the price.
(Photo. H.M.S.O. via 'Britain at Work'.)

The call to 'Take Post' was given on this empty shellcase ' gong' at the Royal Marine ack-ack gun site at Dunes Farm, Tunbridge Wells, and guaranteed to rouse even the deepest sleeper.
(Photo. via R.S. Humphreys.)

Mr A.W.HALL, SEVENOAKS, Kent.	*Civilian - schoolboy at Sundridge.*	Incidents at Sundridge and Dunton Green.

As a small boy of eight-years-old I witnessed, among others, two dramatic V-1 incidents. My home in 1944 was on the Sundridge main road (A25). Our house was situated on a bank to the south of the road, with good views to the south and over the North Downs towards Biggin Hill. Incident one concerns the balloon site south of our house, on the higher ground, known as The Warren. A friend and I were in the fields between our house and The Warren when we heard the sound of a V-1. We looked up to see the doodlebug strike the balloon cable and one wing fell off and fluttered down yards from us; the rest twisted overhead, luckily missing our house, and exploded in a field north of the A.25, known as 'The Lays'. As was the custom, we grabbed a souvenir; in this case the whole V-1 wing, which we somehow dragged home and hid in the shed. We were subsequently 'arrested' by the Police and taken down to another balloon site, east of our house, for a dressing down by an RAF officer. Incident two: I saw a V-1 hit a balloon cable to Dunton Green some two miles from Sundridge. The V-1 spiralled down the cable, causing deaths on the actual balloon site.

Mr M. RHODES, HILDENBOROUGH, Kent.	*Post War Ministry of Supply employee.*	Reconstruction of V-1 at Fort Halstead, Sevenoaks.

I had a couple of weeks leave during August 1944, so I saw quite a few V-1's over Tonbridge, many being chased by the Tempests, but never saw many of them shot down. I did see one that got through, hit a cable of the outer balloon barrage and explode. After the war I joined the Ministry of Supply, later the Ministry of Defence at the R.A.R.D.E. Fort Halstead, Sevenoaks, and in 1968 we held an Open Day. As the V.T. Fuses (Proximity) were developed at the Fort, it was decided to exhibit them in relation to a V-1. A V-1 was procured but was, of course, minus warhead, fuel and battery - I think that it came from an R.O.A.C. depot. It was rather battered, so we set about refurbishing it. One of the air pipes happened to be in the way of a particular job, so the two unions joining the pipes together were unscrewed. It was the wrong side of the reducing valve; as the unions came apart there was a tremendous roar and the chap doing the job was sent flying onto his back, the spanners flying in all directions. The point is that those air bottles had retained their full pressure for nearly 25 years (it had a 1944 date on it). After all the rough treatment it must have received during that period, I think it says something for the German's workmanship!

Mr Bob TOLLETT, DRAYTON, Norfolk.	*Civilian Schoolboy at Tunbridge Wells.*	UXB V-1 at Tunbridge Wells.

In the Summer of 1944 I was eight-years old. One Sunday afternoon over Tunbridge Wells, I saw one doodlebug being pursued by an R.A.F. fighter (a Spitfire?). It disappeared into a cloud, and I got fed up with waiting for it to reappear; then I spotted the doodlebug at only about 20 feet altitude, heading across local sports ground directly towards our house. Panic all round, and as I was bundled down into our basement shelter, I hit my head on the entrance door, and I still have the scar today! We waited for the explosion but none came. I believe that this was the first doodlebug to land without exploding, and later it was displayed at the local Municipal Buildings, collecting money for the Spitfire Fund.

Mr Derek HEARD, MAIDSTONE, Kent.	*Schoolboy in Tonbridge at Slade/Judd Schools.*	Incident on a Sports Ground, Tonbridge.

Although I now live in Maidstone, during the war I lived in Tonbridge and attended the Slade School and then Judd School. I was seven-years-old when the conflict began, my father managed the Dolcis Shoe Co. shop in the High Street and I lived in a flat over the shop with my parents and younger brother. Tonbridge was in the flight path of the German bombers on their way to London and many the dogfight we witnessed overhead during the early days of the war. As children the dangers were not apparent and the debris of shrapnel, cannon shell cases and crashed aircraft became a way of life. However, in 1944, when the flying bombs started the dangers became sudden and unexpected. Again the local children were quickly on the scene to see what we could collect. One particular occasion I well remember was one afternoon, my brother and I were in the Ritz Cinema in Bromley Road, when we heard an almighty bang and we immediately knew a flying bomb had fallen close by; one got to know the sound! We immediately rushed out and found it had crashed in the middle of the Sports Ground. Our first thoughts were to collect what we could and to view the crater and the surrounding damage, fortunately slight, other than damage to one of the nearby cricket pavilions. An hour or so later we wandered home, with the souvenirs, only to be met by our angry and somewhat relieved parents. The blast had blown the shop windows out and shoes had been scattered across the street and my father was busily clearing up the mess. Our parents were upset to think our first thought was to view the crater without showing concern as to how they were and whether our parents were safe. After that close call we boys were packed off to Shropshire with relatives for the Summer Holidays, and only returned when the flying bomb menace had nearly disappeared - and so mysteriously had our box of treasured souvenirs, never to be seen again; probably dispatched to be re-cycled to help the Allied War Effort!

Mr A. Robin ADDEY, TUNBRIDGE WELLS, Kent.	*Civilian - schoolboy ?*	Observer Corps Rocket site at Southborough.

I do not have any personal experiences, beyond seeing a good many pass overhead (time to breathe again!), and the first one that nearly took the roof off this house (metaphorically speaking) pulsating through the night and the one that came down nearby, from which I took part of the tailplane as a souvenir. Between Southborough and Tonbridge is a corner on the main road known as 'Bidborough' Corner. Just beyond on the right hand side, and towards Tonbridge was Nightingale Farm. Just inside the entrance a tiny Observer Corps unit was situated - just two men with a small rocket, to which was attached a flare on a parachute. Their job was to fire this to warn fighters chasing V-1's that they were approaching the barrage balloons. I recall that children used to try to retrieve the parachutes afterwards.

Mr Eddie RUMEL, DEAL, Kent.	*Civilian - evacuee in Tunbridge Wells.*	Disruption to routine at Skinner's School.

I was an evacuee from Lewisham, London with Colfe's Grammar School at Tunbridge Wells in 1944. We shared the buildings of Skinner's School which were, of course, inadequate for both complements of pupils, necessitating our attending for eight periods on a Saturday, and a lot of us travelling around the town during the week, for odd classes at church halls and the Y.M.C.A. I well remember in the Y.M.C.A., when the doodlebug offensive started, we would hear their distinctive engine note overhead. The lessons would continue until the engine cut out, when we would all dive under our desks for cover, and wait about ten seconds for the explosion, then immediately return to our seats for the lesson to continue without any further ado.

Many school children had returned home after the Battle of Britain and the Blitz, but were hastily re-evacuated when the V-1 campaign started.
(Photo. via Kent Messenger via Alistair Bruce.)

TENTERDEN C.D. AREA

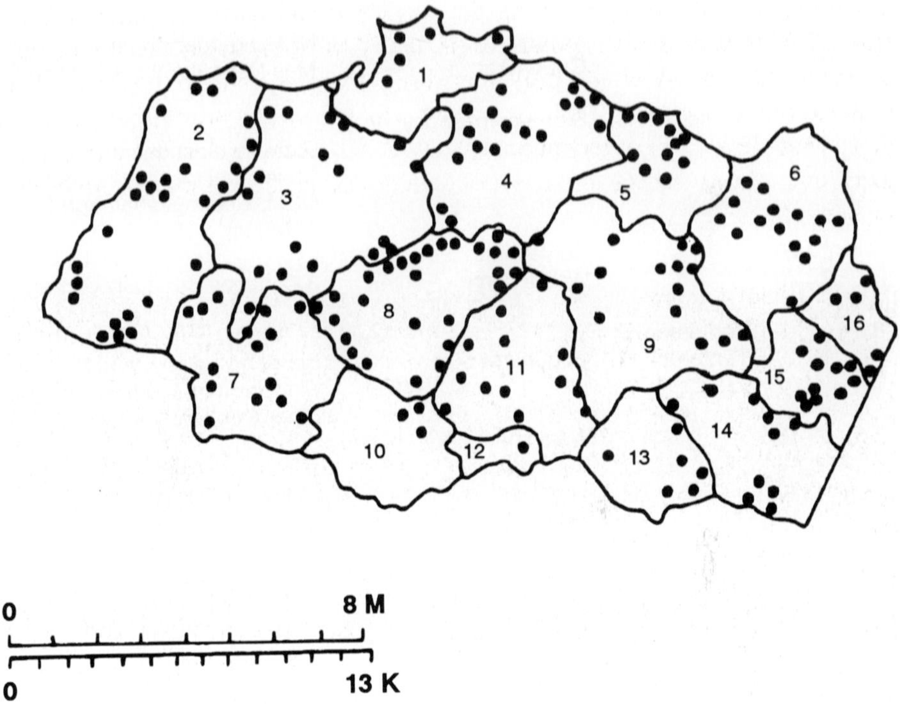

1 FRITTENDEN
2 GOUDHURST
3 CRANBROOK
4 BIDDENDEN
5 HIGH HALDEN
6 WOODCHURCH
7 HAWKHURST
8 BENENDEN
9 BOROUGH OF TENTERDEN
10 SANDHURST
11 ROLVENDEN
12 NEWENDEN
13 WITTERSHAM
14 STONE-CUM-EBONY
15 APPLEDORE
16 KENARDINGTON

TENTERDEN AREA

TENTERDEN BOROUGH and RURAL C.D DISTRICT

Key: AA = Ack-ack fire F = Fighter attack

Date	Time	Area	District	Cause	Location/Incident/Damage
JUNE					
16.6	08.00	Tenterden R	Frittenden		Nr Hungerden Farm
	12.00		Goudhurst	F	Map Ref 139/538 (Kilndown?)
17.6	02.45	Tenterden R	Stone-cum-Ebony	AA	
	05.25		Benenden		Extreme blast damage to BenendenHospital 1 Cottage DEM. 2 cottagesdamage 3 K. 1 Ser. Inj. 5 Sl. Inj.
	17.20		Rolvenden		
	23.20		Woodchurch	AA	3 Cottages Seriously damaged
18.6	01.16	Tenterden B		AA	
	09.10	Tenterden R	Goudhurst		Bedgebury Park - house had windows damaged, was KCC Emergency Hospital
	09.45		Wittersham	F/AA	
	14.40		Rolvenden	F	
	16.50		High Halden		Fell on aerodrome field
	21.10		Sandhurst	F/AA	
19.6	19.50	Tenterden R	Benenden		1 K. 5 Ser. Inj. 1 Sl. Inj.
	23.11				
	23.30		Goudhurst		Fegans Home Ser. dam. 7 Ser Inj 2 Sl Inj
21.6	06.57	Tenterden R	Biddenden		
22.6	05.45	Tenderden R	Hawkhurst	F	150 houses Dam. 6 Sl. Inj.
	05.57		Frittenden	F/AA	
	09.30		Biddenden		
	10.00		Rolvenden	F	
23.6	07.00	Tenterden R	Benenden	F	
	08.05		Goudhurst	F	Opp. 'Post Boys' Hotel on A21, Kilndown
	08.45		Benenden	F	South of Iden Green 16 houses DEM. 2 Ser. Inj. 7 Sl. Inj.

23.6	16.00		Appledore	F	KCC Hostel for agricultural workers DEM 3 Ser. Inj. 4 Sl. Inj.
			Hawkhurst	F	
	21.05		High Halden		On aerodrome
25.6	20.50	Tenterden R	Goudhurst	F	Between Goudhurst & Kilndown. 6 sheep K.
	21.40		Hawkhurst	F	1 Ser. Inj.
	21.55		Hawkhurst	F	2 Sl. Inj.
	23.05		Woodchurch		Susans Hill Farm & 2 Cottages DEM.
	23.10		Biddenden	AA	
26.6	04.00	Tenterden R	High Halden	AA	
	14.53		Kenardington	F	
27.6	02.30	Tenterden R	Goudhurst	AA	Border with Horsmonden and Marden 5 cottages slight damage
	11.35		Biddenden	F/AA	
	11.40		Frittenden	F	
	11.55	Tenterden B		F	
	12.52	Tenterden R	Kenardington	F	
	21.40		Benenden	F	1 house Ser. Dam. 30 Slight dam 3 ser. Inj. 1 Sl. Inj.
28.6	00.15	Tenterden R	Benenden	F	2 houses DEM.
	00.17		Biddenden	F	
	06.30		Goudhurst	F	Between Kilndown and A.21
	07.12		Hawkhurst	F	9 houses Dem. 8 Sl. Inj.
	08.40		Cranbrook	F	Nos 1 & 2 Redwater Cottages DEM
	09.56		Benenden	F	
	09.56	Tenterden B		F	
	12.20	Tenterden R	Stone-cum-Ebony	F	
	12.27		Wittersham	F	
	13.10		Cranbrook	F	Court Stile 5 Sl. Inj.
	16.40		High Halden	F	Nr Ramstile Farm
	21.22		Biddenden	F	Three Chimneys
	22.20		High Halden	F	
	22.55		Rolvenden	AA	
	23.10		?	F	
29.6	12.30	Tenterden R	Benenden		Unexploded on open ground
30.6	07.20	Tenterden R	Biddenden	F	
	15.08		Benenden	AA	
	18.20		Goudhurst	F	Cornfield at Combwell Priory 8 houses slightly damaged

30.6	22.10		Sandhurst	F	
JULY					
01.7	02.15		Hawkhurst	F	Sisley Farm, Cottage DEM.
	04.25		Wittersham	F	
	05.05	Tenterden R	Biddenden	F	
03.7	02.15	Tenterden R	Wittersham		
	16.10		Benenden	F	2 houses Ser. damaged
04.7	10.40	Tenterden R	Benenden	F	
			Rolvenden	F	Farmhouse 3 Sl. Inj.
	23.35		Sandhurst	F	
05.7	01.15	Tenderden B		F	
	12.18	Tenterden R	Cranbrook		Benenden border
	12.30		Appledore	F	
	13.20		Appledore	F/AA	
	14.40		Hawkhurst	F	Beale's Farm House
	19.08		Benenden	F	
07.7	05.50	Tenterden R	Biddenden	F	
	15.20		Appledore	F	
	16.40		Biddenden	F	
	18.30		Tenterden	F	French Hay Farm
	21.00		Kennardington	F	
	22.43		Benenden	F	
	23.35		Stone-cum-Ebony	F	
08.7	22.00	Tenterden R	Rolvenden	F	
09.7	00.15	Tenterden R	Biddenden		
	04.10		Benenden		
	04.45		Stone-cum-Ebony	F	
	21.00		Goudhurst	F	Between Goudhurst & Kilndown, 2 cottages Ser. Dam. 6 Sl. Dam. 1 Sl Inj.
	22.30		Goudhurst	F	Sl. dam. to houses between A21 & Scotney
10.7	14.12	Tenterden R	Benenden	F	30 houses damaged
	19.15		Stone-cum-Ebony	F	
11.7	13.14	Tenterden R	Benenden	F	
	20.55		Wittersham	F	
	20.56		Biddenden	F	Exploded in the air
	21.00		Biddenden	F	1 K. 1 Ser. Inj. 2 Sl. Inj.
12.7	07.20	Tenterden R	Stone-cum-Ebony	F	
	17.50		Benenden	F	
	17.53		Cranbrook	F	

12.7	18.12		Sandhurst	F	
	19.18		Benenden	F	3 K. 3 Ser. Inj.
	21.15	Tenterden B		F	
13.7	10.06	Tenterden R	Goudhurst	F	Nr Bedgebury
	10.08		Woodchurch	F	
	18.58		Hawkhurst	AA	
14.7	18.33	Tenterden B		F	
	18.35	Tenterden R	Woodchurch	F	
16.7	00.10	Tenterden R	Cranbrook	F/AA	
18.7	02.40	Tenterden R	Cranbrook	F	
	18.15		Frittenden	F	2 Sl. Inj.
	22.10		Biddenden	F	
	22.45		Hawkhurst	F	
19.7	10.05	Tenterden B		F	Huson Farm
	10.07	Tenterden R	Rolvenden	F	Little Halden
	11.35		Wittersham	F	
	11.55		Stone-cum-Ebony	F	
	12.40		Rolvenden	F	1 Cottage DEM Fire 2 K 1 Ser Inj 2 Sl In
	13.20		Hawkhurst	F	
	15.30		Biddenden	F	
	16.50		Cranbrook	F	Sissinghurst 1 Sl. Inj.
	18.35		Cranbrook	F	
	23.40		Hawkhurst	F	
	23.40		Kennardington	AA	
20.7	01.10	Tenterden R	Goudhurst	F	Nr Curtisden Green
	01.10		Cranbrook	F	
21.7	15.52	Tenterden R	Goudhurst	F	Damage to farm buildings between Goudhurst and Curtisden Green
	19.28		Goudhurst	F	E. of village Nr A262 nr Peacock PH
	20.20		Smallhythe		Nr Village
22.7	15.45	Tenterden R	Cranbrook	F	Sissinghurst 4 Sl. Inj
	16.45		Goudhurst	F	Nr A21 and Scotney Castle
	18.00		Biddenden	F	
	18.00		Rolvenden		
	19.25		Hawkhurst	F	
	21.00	Tenterden R	Frittenden		
	21.10		Cranbrook	F	
	21.35		Appledore	F	Houses Damaged (see New Romney/Snargate)

22.7	22.00		Woodchurch		Exploded in air
	23.15		Hawkhurst	F	in wood at Conghurst Farm
23.7	06.10	Tenterden R	Sandhurst	F	Unexploded at Scrums Farm
	23.20		Goudhurst	F	Between village & Glassenbury
24.7	00.15	Tenterden R	Appledore	F	Exploded in air
	16.26		Goudhurst	F	Sl. dam. to buildings nr Curtisden Green
	16.33		Benenden	F	1 Sl. Inj
	19.15		Cranbrook	F	Exploded in air, damage to houses
26.7	05.35	Tenterden R	Biddenden	F	Stede Court Farm, to Ledge Place
	06.15		Wittersham	F	Damage to St John the Baptist Church, Smallhythe.
	06.32	Tenterden Boro		F	Nr Lower Knockwood Farm
	14.10			F	St Benedicts Priory & Brunger Farm Dam.
	14.20	Tenterden R	Biddenden	F	
	14.20		Stone-cum-Ebony	F	Reading Street
27.7	21.17	Tenterden R	Woodchurch	F	Exploded in air
	21.20		Goudhurst	F	Nr Kilndown
	21.22			F	Exploded in air
	22.50		Woodchurch	F	Some damage
	22.50	Tenterden Boro		F	In Knock Wood, did not explode
28.7	21.35	Tenterden R	Hawkhurst	F	
	22.37	Tenterden Boro		F	Dam. to property 2 Ser. Inj. 11 Sl. Inj
	22.57	Tenterden R	Appledore		Damage to property, 4 Ser. Inj 2 Sl. Inj
29.7	01.15	Tenterden Boro		AA	
	19.40	Tenterden R	Cranbrook	F	3 Sl. Inj.
	21.30		Kenardington	F	
30.7	00.45	Tenterden R	Cranbrook	F	Exploded in air over town
	13.40		Kennardington	F	
	23.45		Rolvenden		
31.7	14.30	Tenterden R	Goudhurst	F	Farm buildings at Stonecrouch damaged Sl. Dam. to other houses near A.21

AUGUST

01.8	09.50	Tenterden R	Rolvenden		Some damage to houses
03.8	00.40	Tenterden R	Biddenden	AA	Damage to houses
	01.40		Biddenden	AA	Wagstaff Farm, damage to houses
	02.20		Biddenden	AA	Damage to 4 houses 2 Sl. Inj.
	08.03		Cranbrook	F	Windows of M & D bus dam. 1 Ser Inj 19 Sl. Inj.
	08.25		Benenden	F	Damage to Betsons Farm and Mount Pleasant Farm buildings. 1 Sl. Inj.
	12.10		Appledore	F	Exploded in air
	12.45		Benenden	F	Exploded in air - Fighter lost one wing and crashed, pilot was killed
04.8	01.25	Tenterden R	Benenden	F	Damage to farm house & buildings
	02.12		Benenden	F	Damage to Sanatorium
	03.20	Tenterden Boro		AA	
	03.45	Tenterden R	Benenden	F	
	16.00	Tenterden Boro		F	Chicks Farm 1 Sl. Inj
	16.20	Tenterden		F	1 Sl. Inj.
	16.40	Tenterden R	Goudhurst	F	Extensive dam. to property 2 Sl Inj
	16.40		Benenden	F	Dam to cottages 1 Sl. Inj
	18.08	Tenterden Boro		F	
	20.07	Tenterden R	Woodchurch	F	
	20.10		Goudhurst	F	Dam. to Chequer Tree Farm buildings and cottages
05.8	04.30	Tenterden R	Woodchurch	F	Damage to buildings 1 Sl. Inj
	07.00		Cranbrook	F	
	18.53		Woodchurch	F	Haycross & Oakhurst Farms
06.8	03.55	Tenterden B	St Michaels	F	
	03.48	Tenterden R	Cranbrook	F	2 Houses Ser. Dam. 150 Sl. Dam 4 Sl. Inj
	04.43		Woodchurch	F	Slight damage to 12 houses
	05.45		Goudhurst		Nr A21 south of Scotney Castle
	13.25		Woodchurch		Ammunition store set on fire, many houses damaged
	13.30		Goudhurst	F	Bungalow DEM.
07.8	01.40	Tenterden R	Benenden		Exploded in air, Crabtree Farmhouse Dam.
	06.00		Cranbrook	F	
	06.05		Cranbrook	F	Damage to Chequer Tree & High Tilt Farms

07.8	06.08		Cranbrook		Wood
	06.15		Hawkhurst	F	270 houses Dam. 5 Sl. Inj.
	06.15		Goudhurst	F	Nr Combwell Priory, over the A.21
	08.05		Appledore	F	
	23.05		Woodchurch	AA	
08.8	05.05	Tenterden R	Hawkhurst	F	
	05.55		Benenden	F	20 yds from Agricultural Hostel - Sev. damage and to 4 houses. 1 K. 13 Ser. Inj 20 Sl. Inj.
10.8	04.00	Tenterden R	Rolvenden	F	
	04.45		Woodchurch	F	
	21.05		Kenardington	F	
13.8	01.25	Tenterden R	Hawkhurst	F	Parish Church, Vicarage, 25 houses and 3 shops damaged 3 Sl. Inj.
15.8	17.55	Tenterden R	Goudhurst	F	Ladysden Farm damage to Oast House andother houses 2 Sl. Inj.
16.8	18.16	Tenterden R	Stone-cum-Ebony	F	(C.C.type) Knock Farm
	18.16	Tenterden Boro		F	
	19.07	Tenterden R	Cranbrook	F	Little Glassenbury - some damage
	19.45	Tenterden Boro		F	Some damage
	19.50	Tenterden R	Appledore	AA	
17.8	06.10	Tenterden R	Kenardington	F	In marshes
	06.10		Appledore	F	
19.8	06.00	Tenterden R	Cranbrook	F	
	06.42		Rolvenden	F	Damage to 2 cottages
	06.43		Woodchurch	F	
	06.45		Woodchurch	F	
	06.47		Wittersham		
	14.30		High Halden	F	Minor damage 31 houses
	23.30		High Halden	F	
20.8	07.55	Tenterden R	Kenardington		Slight damage to church, farmhouse and cottages
21.8	04.30	Tenterden R	Woodchurch		Damage to farmhouse
	13.15		Kenardington	AA	Damage to cottage and farmhouse

24.8	07.30	Tenterden R	Stone-cum-Ebony		
	07.35		Stone-cum-Ebony	F	
	08.12		Woodchurch	F	
	21.10		Frittenden		Several houses damaged
	21.45		High Halden		Damage to 12 houses
27.8	06.37	Tenterden R	Woodchurch	F	
	06.38		Rolvenden	F	Exploded in air
	07.10	Tenterden Boro		F	Damage to property 3 Sl. Inj.
	07.10	Tenterden Boro		F	Severe damage to house & farm buildings
28.8	14.25	Tenterden R	Woodchurch	F	Shirley Moor
	14.35		Stone-cum-Ebony	F	
	15.00		Newenden	F	Damage to property
	16.25			F	Damage to buildings 2 Ser. Inj. at Merrington
	17.00		Frittenden	F	
	17.35		Wittersham	F	
	18.35			F	
29.8	11.55	Tenterden R	Cranbrook	F	
	12.50		High Halden	F	1 Sl. Inj.
	16.50		Stone-cum-Ebony	AA	

American Thunderbolt fighters lined up at Woodchurch A.L.G. wait for the signal to take-off. Although not directly involved with defences against V-1's, the 412th Fighter Bomber Group did manage to down three near Dover. (Photo. Col. William Mather.)

Mr W. GOODWIN, HAWKHURST, Kent.	*Apprentice wireman Weald Electricity Supply Co.*	Incidents at Hawkhurst.

22.06.44 05.45am.

One morning, while I was still in bed, I heard a flying bomb and then the engine stopped and I heard an explosion. It had landed on the wall surrounding the Hall House kitchen garden, demolishing the wall but did not do a lot of other damage, apart from the blast which damaged some houses, including ours, although it was in the valley, one field away from where it landed. Our roof tiles were stripped off and we were covered in plaster from the ceiling and were left looking up at the sky. One of my father's goats was tethered about thirty yards from where the V-1 landed, but when I went to see if she was all right, she was calmly grazing, with only a scratch on her nose. The pulse tube from the doodlebug had been blown right over her and had landed in the middle of the field. (This V-1 was shot down by a fighter; approx. 150 houses were damaged and six people were slightly injured.)

13.08.44 01.25am.

I have a friend, Mike Russ, who lived at the end of the churchyard, and he still lives there. A V-1 was shot down by a fighter and landed in the churchyard, the church, the vicarage, and the graveyard were badly damaged. As well as three shops in the village, some 25 houses were also damaged, including Mike's, which was only 200 yards away, and was damaged by a chunk of gravestone. Other incidents which I remember include one flying bomb which hit trees in Horns Road, just as a lady opened her front door to see what was going on; I think that she was killed. I heard that another had fallen on a lorry at the nearby Army Camp when some soldiers and children were sheltering under it. I do remember seeing one V-1 which was tipped over by a Spitfire, that was while I was working at the 'Little Fowlers' Nursing Home.

Mr John NYE, TUNBRIDGE WELLS, Kent.	*Civilian - Schoolboy* *Angley Park, Cranbrook.*	Incident at Court Style, Cranbrook.

13.10pm 28.06.44.

I was pushing my bike up Windmill Hill, Cranbrook on my way home to lunch from school. Being a keen spotter, I stopped to look back when I heard the intensifying sound of a doodlebug. This one was being chased by a Meteor. About level with the windmill the pilot scored a direct hit and one of the wings fell off the Bug. This meant that it would land fairly close, as it seemed to be pointed straight at me. Without more ado, I dropped my bike and dived into a ditch which was luckily dry, opposite the steep slope that goes up to 'The Windmill' pub. I knew I should put my elbows on the ground and cover my ears and head. The wait seemed interminable, but was presumably it was only a few seconds. There was a loud explosion. Scrambling out of the ditch I saw a cloud of smoke rising in the direction of Court Style. With a quick "Are you all right?" to a girl, who had done the same thing 100 yards further up the hill, I cycled off to view the victory. The doodlebug had landed in Cranbrook Town's cricket field but there was little to see except a large hole, although I later learned a horse had been killed. (There were in fact five people slightly injured.) One took this sort of thing for granted in those days and being a hungry sixteen-year-old, now late for lunch, I cycled off home. We lived in Angley Park and I was met by my anxious mother, who had also heard the bang and finding me 10 minutes later for lunch - feared the worst. Undressing that night, I found a minute tear in the ankle of my sock and the tiniest scratch showing blood. The Home Guard had placed some barbed wire in the ditch in 1940 and by now it was well overgrown and invisible, so perhaps I can claim to have suffered the slightest injury from a V-1 incident?

Col William MATHER, RICHARDSON, Texas.	*Pilot - 411th Fighter Sqd* *373rd Fighter Group* USAAF.	Incidents near Woodchurch ALG.

When we were flying, we were told to keep the 'ell out of the way' of the R.A.F. Spitfires and Typhoons, which were much lighter and more manoeuvrable than our lumbering 'Jugs' (P-47 Thunderbolts). But the temptation was great, because it seemed that the vast majority of the beastly things came directly over our fragile tents. We did chase a few while airborne, but the R.A.F. fighters let us know they didn't like our intrusion, and we knew for a certainty that the ack-ack boys would gleefully shoot at anything that moved, so we did not press the issue. Nevertheless, our squadron scored on three, near Dover. On the night of June 13th 1944, with a 'left handed' bunch walking back from Ashford, 'old Adolph' unleashed a swarm of his noisiest aircraft, which began passing directly overhead, each with a strange glowing light marking its passage (the first V-1's, although we didn't know what they were at the time). Here they came, buzzing and clattering in from the West and suddenly the peaceful Kentish countryside became alive with a storm of anti-aircraft weapons, all firing at once. You know, there is one thing you can say about the ack-ack boys, no matter what flag they salute, they never learn to lead! As pilots, we had learned deflection shooting, so we were discussing, with academic vigour, the common tendency of all ground troops to shoot behind the target instead of ahead of it, being all together too noisy, making loud and derisive comments about the waste of ammunition. We were overheard! Out of the bushes beside the road, came a bullish roar: "You bloody *****, ***** Yanks, get your ***** arses out of our field of fire!!!" and not fifty feet from where we were standing, an entire battery of rather largish pieces began whanging away over our heads; we lost no time in following orders. Afterwards though, we seven or eight people were all struck by the same thought. Why weren't those 40mm Bofors guns tracking the targets, instead of coming round in our direction? Nah..h..h.. they wouldn't... would they? HMMMMM!!!

Mrs Joyce SMITH, FELIXSTOWE, Suffolk.	*LACW 'Y' service D/F Station at Wittersham.*	Incidents linked at A.S.R. rescues.

Our Direction Finding station was at Wittersham, between Tenterden and Rye and was connected to the Kenley Sector Operations Room, and in 1944 to Biggin Hill S.O.R., but my wartime diary tells me we were also occasionally connected to Dover. The R.A.F Controller operating from Dover was Squadron Leader Hunter, who managed to produce an expertise in ground control interception that was never matched by any other R.A.F. Control Centre. We listened to all the intercom between the Controllers and pilots and the bearings we took on their aircraft in distress enabled the Walrus amphibians and High Speed Launches to find their exact location -

the initial key factor in the team effort of Air Sea Rescue. We logged 'May Day' calls of pilots ditching in the Channel and could listen to conversations when they were airborne. As they sometimes used nicknames on the air, we recognised some of them by their voices, especially the Canadians! When we took over at Wittersham we found that the men whom we replaced had 'sabotaged' the equipment by turning back all the dials and hiding things. They were not keen to see us take over as they were to be posted abroad; the first case of 'male chauvinism'? I can remember listening in to pilots as they chased doodlebugs'; and one of the V-1s exploded over our billets and ruined a colleague's washing. We had to exchange items when 'worn out' and we would help this along by pushing our fingers through things that were wearing thin. I often wondered what the Clothing Exchange Clerk said when told the reason for my friend's claim for replacement garments.

Mrs Margery ISLEMONGER, APPLEDORE, Kent.	*Student - visits home to Appledore.*	Incident at Manclark Cottage, 22.7.44.

I was a student at Bedford in 1944 and returned home at the end of July. I was just in time for the evening attack. It was the turn of the 'Manclark Menace'. My stepmother and I were looking out from an upstairs window. Suddenly the doodlebug (which was low) started heading for the ground. "Mummy, Mummy," I said, "quick, get down!" "No, Darling," she said, "the light always goes out first," so I just grabbed her and pulled her down; the Doodle Bug landed; the cottage rose and settled, shedding a few tiles, but all windows were open; so peace again. There was considerable damage to another bungalow, a farm house and the Victoria pub, but fortunately, no lives were lost.

Mr V.A.VICKERS, SURBITON, Surrey.	*Owner - Children's Farm, St Michaels.*	Incident at Children's Farm, Tenterden 6.8.44.

My family, the Honeysetts, have farmed in this area since 1880. My Grandfather, Jabez Honeysett, bought Children's Farm in Norton Lane and its 60 acres in 1912. But on 6th August 1944 it was demolished by the explosion of a doodlebug, the only bit left being the cellar. My two aunts, May and Ennie Honeysett, were living there when this doodlebug struck but they both had miraculous escapes as they were in the cellar and crawled out through the rubble. The reason that there was such widespread damage was the fact that the V-1 hit a tree adjacent to the house and the blast was accordingly spread in all directions above ground. The great good fortune was the fact that this meant that the house merely collapsed, and my uncle and aunts, sheltering in the cellar, were relatively unharmed. I understand that this was the only farm in Kent where a doodlebug demolished, not only the house, but also all the farm buildings and destroyed all the farm equipment, i.e. the stables, corn-store, barn, cowshed, pig-styes, wagon lodge; inclusive of the tractors, carts and even the hand tools.

Mr R.A.PUNNETT, DOVER, Kent.	*Driver-mechanic with* *A.O.R.G. Camber Sands.*	Plotting V-1, ack-ack and radar tracking.

I believe that a special unit, the Army Operations Research Group, was formed specifically to study the flight, trajectory, speed, etc. of rockets which the powers-that-be were clearly anticipating a long time prior to their first incursion into this country as the V-1. As a driver-mechanic, I was seconded from my searchlight unit to the A.O.R.G., to drive and maintain a 3-ton Bedford; this vehicle was virtually a mobile office, with dials and an overhead camera; the unit being connected by cables to radar and predictors on ack-ack gun sites. During an action, it was possible to take a constant photograph of the dials, which of course, corresponded with those of the predictor and radar information. From these photographs a graph was produced; showing the exact location of a given target, and the point at which the shell was predicted to explode, plus other information such as speed of the target, trajectory, etc.

During the 18 months I spent with this unit of three (an officer, a sergeant and myself) we travelled from Norfolk to Southampton (where I saw my first V-1) then to Camber Sands, where they came in thick and fast. The R.A.F. downed most, and it was a thrill to see fighters sweep on the target and see the marauder explode in mid-air. I have no doubt that the unit did play a significant part in the combat and the understanding of these rocket propelled missiles.

Due to anti-aircraft fire, fighter interceptions and the balloon barrage around S.E. London, many V-1's fell, to leave their mark on the countryside of Kent, typified by damage to this oast at Tudeley, near Tonbridge. (Photo. Kent Messenger via Alistair Bruce.)

Fighter Direction aerial display with buildings associated with radar used during the V-1 campaign. Coastal Radar sets in Kent were modified to give early warning of approaching V-l's before they crossed the coast.
(Photo. via Imperial War Museum CH15204)

Ground Control Interceptor Station (Radar) with associated buildings. While serving with No. 85 Mosquito Squadron, F/Off Hackney and his fellow crew members visited Sandwich M.E.W.S. Radar station to watch their colleagues intercept V-l's over the Channel by night.
(Photo. Imperial War Museum CH15183.)

F/OFF Tom HACKNEY, DEAL, Kent.	*Assistant Controller at R.A.F. Biggin Hill Operations Room.*	Background to V-1 first attacks and diversion tactics.

Before I was fully fit to return to duty, I was offered the post of Assistant Controller at Biggin Hill Operations Room, where I served from 19.1.44 to 3.9.44. It wasn't an essential post, but a very useful one for people like myself who were convalescent, to help out where they could. It was realised that the Controller could always do with some help when things are busy. He was up on the dais with his Opp P.1 who is usually a WAAF who assisted him on the secretarial side, but the value of somebody who flies and knows all about it was certainly a lot of help to him. I wasn't personally responsible for controlling interceptions, but was in a position to advise if he required assistance. Below us there were about half a dozen WAAF plotters, with long sticks around the table, who moved the symbols across the table, which had a map of the Biggin Hill sector. But we were not at R.A.F. Biggin Hill at all, but down the road on the outskirts of Bromley in a house that had formerly been owned by the banker Sir Montague Norman. This had been completely gutted and the operations room had been constructed within the shell; but if had been hit, it would have collapsed completely. I was there on the night when the 'Buzz Bomb' attacks started. It all started without 'Buzz Bombs' at all. I was on duty one night and we had two or three Messerschmitt Me 410s coming over on scattered raids round about Kent. These were followed by a report from the Observer Corps, at Malling or somewhere near Maidstone, of a bomb being dropped when there were no aircraft in the air at all. We checked this with them, but they were convinced it had come from a bomber. About half-an-hour later another one arrived, quite a few miles short of the first, and it was then that we started to get suspicious. They were, in fact, very long distance shells being fired from somewhere in the Boulogne area. There was only this one effort, five or six shells, each one falling further back into Kent as the rifling of the gun barrel wore down. All this was part of V-1, a diversion tactic! The next night the first of the Buzz Bombs came over, and one was reported on the Chislehurst golf links, where it bounced along on the ground getting gradually lower and lower before it eventually exploded. Our W.A.A.F.'s lived in the Chislehurst caves for a bit, because quite frequently when they had their own quarters, after they had come off duty and went back, it was to find broken windows and everything in a mess, so they were given the opportunity to go into the caves. We had orders issued to us, long before it happened, giving instructions as to what we should do when the code word 'Diver' was issued. But when it came though, do you think we could find that piece of paper; it did turn up fairly quickly in the end, but there was a bit of a panic at first. Then after that, they started coming over quite regularly. I think some 250 fell within a five mile radius of our Operations Room, some only a couple hundred yards at the back. When this happened everybody in the control room started to get tense as we could hear the sound of a V-1's engine approaching, but so long as it kept going everyone then relaxed again. It was a bit terrifying actually! One of the more frightening ones I remember was when the WAAF girls were plotting one coming across the Channel and it was heading directly for Biggin Hill. As well as 'Buzz Bombs' there were other things going on to be plotted as well. I had to admire those girls as they could see exactly what we could above. One of our night fighters had shot it up and reported this to us, but it hadn't crashed but was still going although it was on fire. On the map it was shown as coming right up to us. There was a door onto a flat roof from the back of the controller's dais, so I nipped out of this and as it was dusk I could see it. It was glowing red hot, but still going very slowly as the gyros were still controlling it and just as it reached us it had started to roll from side to side. However, it passed by and fell in one of the main streets in the middle of Bromley. I went down to look at the damage, which did not look all that much, but the blast had been ricocheting, from side to side, breaking windows on one side of the street but not opposite.

De Havilland Mosquitos were flown by No. 85 Squadron from West Malling while on patrol at night over the Channel and Thames estuary. At night they circuited twin vertical searchlights while awaiting their quarry.
(Photo. via R.M. Hackney.)

Some aircraft casualties during the V-1 campaign in Kent

List not complete as some aircraft did not return for reasons unknown

17.6.44 Spitfire IX MH852 of 229 Sqd - missing from anti-V-1 patrol.

22.6.44 Tempest V JN806 of 486 Sqd based Newchurch - F.O T.M Fenton safe. Belly landed and written off after undercarriage jammed on landing at Newchurch.

23.6.44 Tempest V JN732 of 3 Sqd based Newchurch - F/Sgt M.J.A Rose crashed Brenzett. Not known if he was hurt and there is a possibility that the date was the 24th.

28.6.44 Tempest V JN829 of 406 Sqd - P.O F.B.Lawless safe. The V-l exploded damaging aircraft had to forced land at Collyers Farm, East Guildford, E. Sussex.

29.6.44 Spitfire XIV of 322 Sqd based West Malling - F/Sgt De Vries unhurt. Hit by own AA on Diver patrol, holes in cowling and starboard aileron lost. Forced landed Kingsnorth. Dam Cat B.

30.6.44 Tempest V JN810 of 486 Sqd based Newchurch. W.O S.J. Short safe. Damaged by debris from V-1 and crash landed near Newchurch. Damaged beyond repair.

01.7.44 Tempest V JN765 of 3 Sqd based Newchurch. F.O G.K Kosh killed when chasing a V-1 and crashed SW of Rye, E. Sussex.

03.7.44 Spitfire XIV of 382 Sqd based West Malling - Shot down a V-1 which exploded in the air and was scorched by the explosion.

04.7.44 Spitfire XIV of 322 Sqd based West Malling. F.O Speetjens O.K Engine cut out after attacking V-1 and forced landed in wheat field near Hever.

04.7.44 Tempest V JN820 of 486 Sqd based Newchurch. P.O S.S.Williams safe. Returned to base from V-1 patrol, crashed on landing & written off.

07.7.44 Spitfire XIV of 322 Sqd based West Malling. F.O Burgwal unhurt Aircraft scorched by exploding V-1 and forced landed Ashford.

09.7.44 Spitfire IX MH826 of 274 Sqd based W. Malling. P.O. N.J.Purce killed and buried Maidstone. Flew into balloon barrage having missed airfield, hit cable and crashed at Wrotham Heath.

11.7.44 Mosquito XIII MM547 of 409 Sqd Missing from V-1 night patrol.

12.7.44 Mustang III FB378 0f 316 Sqd based Friston. Caught in blast of exploding V-1 and the aircraft abandoned. Location not certain. F/Sgt Pietrazic baled out unhurt.

18.7.44 Mosquito XIII MM511 96 Sqd based Ford. Sqd Ldr Parker-Rees & Fl. Lt Bennett picked up by HMS Obedient after 6 hours; shot down in Channel by friendly AA fire whilst attacking V-1.

18.7.44 Beaufighter 1F R2080 of 51 OTU - Hit anti-V-1 Balloon cable, port engine caught fire, a/c crashed Werke Farm, Kingsdown.

24.7.44 Tempest V JN860 of 486 Sqd based Newchurch F.Lt N.J Powell safe. Engine cut and forced landed Snargate. A/c written off.

26.7.44 Mosquito XIII MM468 of 96 Sqd missing from anti- V-1 patrol over the Channel.

26.7.44 Mosquito XIX MM655 of 157 Sqd based West Malling, missing on anti V-1 patrol.

27.7.44 Tempest V RJ545 of 56 Sqd based Newchurch. F.Lt R.K.Dean OK Crashed and written off when engine failed and forced landed.

27.7.44 Typhoon 1B MN156 of 137 Sqd collided with MN596 on anti V-1 patrol and both crashed at Denton Court.

29.7.44 Mustang III of 306 Sqd - Shot down by own AA while chasing a V-1 three miles south of Hastings, Sussex.

03.8.44 Spitfire XIV 91 Sqd based West Malling. F.Lt Maridor killed Shot down V-1 which exploded in air, fighter lost wing and crashed at Benenden.

04.8.44 Spitfire IX NH466 of 1 Sqd based Lympne. W.O J.W. McKenzie slightly injured. Belly landed near Lympne after engine had failed while on V-1 patrol.

07.8.44 Mosquito XIX MM649 239 Sqd. Flew into ground while on night anti V-1 patrol. Crashed Frinningham Manor.

15.8.44 Meteor I EE226 of 616 based Manston. F/Sgt D.A Begg killed. Attempted landing at High Halden ALG; lost in bad visibility but crashed on approach.

17.8.44 Spitfire XII MB854 of 41 Sqd based Lympne. Shot down V-1 and suffered engine failure but landed safely at Brookland, Romney Marsh.

17.8.44 Tempest V JN805 of 486 Sqd based Newchurch. F/Sgt J.W Waddel killed. Flew into ground in low cloud; crashed at Woodchurch.

20.8.44 Mustang III FB395 129 Sqd based Brenzett. Spun into ground and destroyed while on anti-V-1 patrol; crashed near Ashford.

23.8.44 Tempest V EJ635 of 486 Sqd based Newchurch. F.Lt E.W. Tanner safe; overturned on landing from anti V-1 patrol, Newchurch.

03.9.44 Tempest V JN816 of 56 Sqd based Newchurch. F.O R.V Dennis OK Engine failed on V-1 patrol, forced landed near Brookland, Romney Marsh.

The many forced landings by R.A.F. aircraft in the Kent Countryside aroused the curiosity of the local youngsters, who would appear at the scene almost before pilots had landed.
(Photo K.A.H.R.S. Archives - W.Smith Collection)

Some extracts from the Operations Record Book of No 486 Sqd
based at Newchurch during the period of the flying Bomb attacks

17.6.44 P.O. Danzey in Tempest JN809 shot down 'Diver' nr Faversham

18.6.44 F.O. Powell in JN804 shot down Diver off Dungeness.
F/Sgt Eagleson in JN811 shot down Diver over Tonbridge
P.O. Danzey in JN797 shot down Diver N. of Tonbridge
F.O. J.G.Wilson in JN809 shot down Diver near Dartford.
F/Sgt Eagleson in JN804 destroyed Diver 5/10 miles North of Newchurch.
F/Sgt B.M. Hall in JN809 shot down Diver SE of Sevenoaks which fell near a searchlight site

22.6.44 F.Lt McCan in JN821 destroyed Diver 4 miles N of Newchurch

25.6.44 F.O Williams in JN758 destroyed Diver North of Newchurch
F.O R.J.Cammock destroyed Diver South of Maidstone in JN804
W.O Sheddan in JN854 destroyed Diver 2 miles N of Newchurch

03.7.44 F.O W.L Miller on anti Diver patrol had engine failure, he abandoned aircraft and baled out, landing near Horsmonden, slightly injured in ankle and shoulder. He was treated by the local Doctor who sent in a bill for £1.1.0 (£1.05p)

04.7.44 F.O H.M. Mason in JN805 shot down Diver South of Brookland

24.7.44 F.Lt L.F.Appleton in JN863 shot down Diver 5 miles WSW of Canterbury at 05.26.

04.8.44 P.O K.A.Smith in JN821 shot down one Diver 9 miles North of Tunbridge Wells at 19.00; another near Tunbridge Wells at 19.20 and a third near Maidstone at 19.25.

From 16.6.44 to 4.9.44 No 486 Sqd flew 2443 Anti Diver sorties and shot down 241 Flying Bombs.

Facsimile of News Bulletin issued to No 150 Wing at Newchurch

No. 150 WING NEWS BULLETIN. 85 GROUP. NO. 30

Operations for 19th & 20th June, 1944, by Newchurch Squadrons.

No. 3 SQUADRON. 19/06/44.

43 sorties were flown against pilot-less aircraft. The following pilots made claims:-

F/O Barkcley	1½	destroyed
F/O Edwards	1	”
F/Lt Moore	3	”
F/O Kosh	1	”
P/O Feldman	1½	”
P/O Whitman	1	”
W/Cdr.Beaumont	1	” (flying 3 Sqdn a/c)

NO. 56 SQUADRON. 19/06/44.

30 sorties were flown including a Beach Head patrol of 8 aircraft a Shipping Lane patrol of 4 aircraft, 4 Weather Recces and 3 Convoy Escorts.

When returning from the Beach Head Patrol F/Sgt. Hughes in “T” shot down a “Doodle-bug” which exploded in the sea off Beachy Head. F/Lt Bateman-Jones “P”, Sgt Wydle “W”, F/Sgt. Miller “K”, F/O. Dean “S” and F/Sgt. Shaw “K” all had squirts during the day, but were unable to catch them.

NO. 486 SQUADRON. 19/6/44.

38 sorties were flown by the Squadron. 5 divers were destroyed and several damaged and probably destroyed.

No. 3 SQUADRON. 20/6/44.

30 sorties against pilot-less aircraft were sent up by the Squadron and the following pilots claim successes:-

F/Lt Umbers,	P/O Feldman (2)
P/O Slade-Betts,	P/O Wingate,
W/O Adcock,	F/O Kosh,
F/Sgt. Smith,	F/O Clapperton

One each, destroyed

Nearly 200 sorties have been made by the Squadron in the last four days.

Apart from very minor defects the aircraft have given no trouble and have responded to everyone of the very heavy demands made on them.
The Squadron Commander congratulates the ground crews who have enabled the pilots to score such conspicuous success.

NO. 56 SQUADRON. 20/6/44

8 aircraft provided assault cover in the Beach Head area in the early morning and in the evening. 4 aircraft patrolled along the Eastern Shipping Lane at the same times.

NO. 486 SQUADRON. 20/6/44

During the day ''Doodle-bug'' hunting continued with success for P/O Danzey, F/Lt McCaw and F/Sgt Stafford.
A total of 27 sorties were flown.

THE ABOVE INFORMATION IS SECRET AND MUST NOT BE DISCUSSED OFF CAMP, OR COMMUNICATED TO ANYONE.

Pilot Officer 'Buck; Feldman (Canadian) flying Tempests with 3 Squadron (RAF) at Newchurch ALG, photographed a few days after receiving his DFC on 2nd July 1944.
(Photo. S.B. Feldman.)

Facimilie of Combat Report for first V-1 downed by a jet aircraft

<u>S E C R E T</u>

<u>CONSOLIDATED DIVER REPORT</u>
<u>NO.616 SQD.</u>
<u>R.A.F STATION MANSTON.</u>

<u>F./O T.D. DEAN</u>

At 1545 hours I was "scrambled" (under Kingsley 11 Control) for Anti Diver Patrol between Ashford and Robertsbridge.

Flying at 4,500 feet 340 m.p.h I.A.S. I saw one Diver 4 to 5 Miles south east of Tenterden flying at 1000 feet on a course of 330° estimated speed of 365 m.p.h (16.16 hours)

From 2½ miles behind the Diver I dived down from 4,500 feet at 470 m.p.h. Closing in to attack I found my 4 x 20 m.m guns would not fire owing to a technical trouble now being investigated. I then flew my Meteor alongside the Diver for approx 20 - 30 seconds. Gradually I manoeuvred my wing tip a few inches under the wing of the Diver, then pulling my aircraft upwards and sharply I turned the Diver over on its back and sent it diving to earth approx. 4 miles south of Tonbridge.

On return to Manston I was informed that R.O.C had confirmed one Diver had crashed at position given by me.

This is the first pilotless aircraft to be destroyed by a jet propelled aircraft.

<u>Claim 1 "Diver" Destroyed</u>
Date 4. 8. 44
Sqdn. 616
Aircraft Meteor Mark 1
Pilot F/O. Dean
Call-sign HUGO 24.
Time up 1554 hrs. Time down 16.35 hrs.
Weather 3/10 cloud at 5,000 ft.
visibility good. Sgd. *T.D.Dean* F/O

Kent-based Fighter Squadrons Involved in the Flying Bomb Attacks

Fighter Pilots who shot down five or more Flying Bombs

<u>No. 1 Squadron</u> - Spitfire IXB based at Detling/Lympne/Detling/Manston

P.O D. Day	Br	6

<u>No. 3 Squadron</u> - Tempest V based at Newchurch

Sqdn Ldr J. Berry	Br	61½ (also with 501 Sqd)
Sqdn Ldr R.Van Lierde	Belg	40
Sqdn Ldr A.R Umbers	NZ	28
F.O R.W.Cole	Br	21⅔
F.Lt A.R.Moore	Br	21½
F.O R.H Clapperton	Br	21
Sqd Ldr R.Dryland	Br	21
P.O K.G.Slade-Betts	Br	20
P.O H.R.Wingate	Br	17½
F.O R.E.Barckley	Br	12
F/Sgt M.J.A Rose	Br	12
F/Sgt H.G.Bailey	Br	11½
P.O S.B.Feldman	USA	9¾
F/Sgt B.J.MacKerras	Br	8¾
P.O M.J.Edwards	Br	8¾
Sqd Ldr A.S.Dredge	Br	6
P.O L.G.Everson	Br	5½
F/Sgt R.Pottinger	Br	5½
F.Lt G.A.Whitman	Br	5¼

<u>No. 41 Squadron</u> - Spitfire XII based at West Malling/Lympne

F.O M.A.L Balasse	Br	7
F.Lt T. Spencer	Br	6

<u>No. 56 Squadron</u> - Tempest V based at Newchurch

F/Sgt H.Shaw	Br	9½
F.O W.R.MacLaren	Br	5½
F/Sgt Wylde	Br	5½
Sqdn Ldr A.R.Hall	Br	5

No. 91 Squadron - Spitfire XIV/XIB based at West Malling/Biggin Hill

Sqd Ldr N.A. Kynaston	Br	17
F.Lt R.Nash	Br	16 ½
F.O E.Topham	Br	15
F.O H.D.Johnson	Br	11
Capt J.M.Maridor *	Fr	11
F.O Cruikshank	Br	9 ½
F.Lt P.M.Bond	Br	9
Lt H.F De Bordas	Fr	8 ½
F.O A.R.L.Elcock	Br	8
F.Lt W.C.Marshall	Br	8
F.Lt H.B.Moffett	Br	7
F.O R.A.McPhie	Br	6 ½
F.O K.R.Collier	Br	6
Sqdn Ldr J.W.P Draper	Can	6
F.O J.A.Faulkner	Br	5 ½

* Capt Maridor was killed when he either rammed a Flying Bomb trying to prevent it hitting the Military Hospital at Benenden or was blown up in the explosion when he shot it down on 3.8.44

No. 129 Squadron - Mustang III based at Brenzett.

F.O J.Hartley	Br	11
F.Lt D.F.Ruchwaldy	Br	10
F.Lt R.G Kleinmayer	NZ	7 ½
P.O E.W.Edwards	Br	6
F.O Osborne	Br	5

No. 137 Squadron - Typhoon 1B based at Manston

F.Lt N.Sames	Br	5

No. 157 Squadron - Mosquito XIX based at West Malling.

Wing Cmdr J.G.Benson	Br	6
Sqd Ldr J.H.M.Chisholm	Br	5
F.Lt J.O.Matthews	Br	5

No. 165 Squadron - Spitfire IXB based at Detling/Lympne/Detling

F.O C.H.Lawson	Br	6

No. 306 Squadron - Mustang III based at Brenzett

F/Sgt S.Rudowski	Pol	9
F.Lt J.Seikierski	Pol	9
F/Sgt J. Zalenski	Pol	8 ½
F.Lt A.Beyer	Pol	5
F.Lt W. Klawe	Pol	5
F/Sgt W.Nowoczyn	Pol	5

No. 313 Squadron - Mustang III based at Brenzett

F/Sgt T. Janowski	Pol	6 ¾
F/Sgt K. Suwek	Pol	5 ½

No. 316 Squadron - Mustang III based at West Malling

W.O T. Szymanski	Pol	8
F/Sgt A. Pietrazak	Pol	7
Sgt J. Mielnieki	Pol	6
F.Lt A. Cholajda	Pol	5 ½
F.Lt L. Majewski	Pol	5 ½
F.Lt T. Szymankiewicz	Pol	5 ½
W.O C. Barllomiejczyk	Pol	5

No. 322 Squadron - Spitfire XIV/LFIXE based at West Malling/Biggin Hill

Lt Burgwal	Dut	21
F.Lt J.L Plesman	Dut	12
Lt J. Van Arkel	Dut	12
F.O J.Jengbloed	Dut	9 ½
F.Lt L.C.M Van Bedenborg	Dut	8
F/Sgt M.J. Janssen	Dut	6

No. 486 Squadron - Tempest V based at Newchurch.

F.Lt O.D.Eagelson	NZ	21
F.O R.J.Cammock	NZ	20 ½
F.Lt J.H.McCaw	NZ	19 ½
Sqdn Ldr J.R.Cullen	NZ	16
F.O R.J.Danzey	NZ	11
Sqdn Ldr H.N.Sweetman	NZ	10 ½
F.Lt F.B.Lawless	NZ	10

No. 486 Squadron cont.

F.O B.J.O'Connor	NZ	8 ½
F.O G.J.Hooper	NZ	8
W.O W.A. Kalka	NZ	8
F.O K.A.Smith	NZ	8
F.Lt J.H.Stafford	NZ	8
F.Lt S.S.Williams	NZ	8
F.Sgt B.M.Hall	NZ	7 ½
Sqdn Ldr C.J.Shedan	NZ	7 ½
P.O R.B. Bremner	NZ	7
F.O W.A.Hart	NZ	7
F.O W.L.Miller	NZ	7
P.O K.McCarthy	NZ	6
P.O W.A.L. Trott	NZ	6
F.O H.M. Mason	NZ	5 ½
F.Lt N.J. Powell	NZ	5
F/Sgt S.J. Short	NZ	5

No. 501 Squadron - Tempest V based at Manston.

Sqdn Ldr A.Parker-Rees	Br	9 (also with 96 Sqd)
F.O R.C Deleuze	Br	8
F.Lt G.L.Bonham	Br	8
Flt.Off B.F.Miller	USA	5

(the following listed with other squadrons also served with No. 501)

Sqd Ldr J.Berry	(3 Sqd)
F.Lt F.L.Williams	(605 Sqd)

No. 605 Squadron - Mosquito VI based at Manston.

Fl Lt J.G.Musgrave	Br	12
F.Lt E.L.Williams	Br	12 (also with 501 Sqd)
F.O. B.G.Bensted	Br	8
F.Lt G.G.Wright	Br	8
F.Lt R.G.Walton	Br	6

No. 610 Squadron - Spitfire XIV based at West Malling/Lympne.

Sqd Ldr R.A.Newbery	Br	7
F.Lt J.B.Shepherd	Br	7

N.B The following personnel were also involved :-

Wing Cmdr R.P.Beaumont	Br	32
F.Lt B.M.Madden	NZ	6
W.O S.Z Bedowski	Pol	5
Wing Comdr R.T.H.Gibbs	Br	5
F.O P.S.Leggatt	Can	5
F.O B.Pagram		5
F.Lt E.W.Tanner	NZ	5
Wing Comdr. P.D. Thompson	Br	5
F.Lt J.G.Worthington	Br	5
F.O D.J.Wright	Can	5

On site instruction on the flying bomb being undertaken at Newchurch by members of No. 3 Squadron. (left to right F/Sgt Rose; F/O Barckley; P/O Dryland and P/O Slade-Betts.
(Photo via S.B. Feldman.)

INDEX

ILLUSTRATIONS

Royal Navy Launch (ML445) operated from Dover and Ramsgate in mid-Channel to warn fighter by a direct radio link of potential V-1 targets. The special aerial was obliterated by the censor in this photograph.
(Photo. via Norman Gilbraith.)

The Cross of Sacriface erected in Lenham cemetery commemorating the young R.E.M.E. lads who were victims of a rogue V-1 that fell on their camp at Newlands Stud, Charing, early on the morning of 24th June 1944. The wrought iron entrance gates were erected as their memorial, together with the two plaques on the pillars - one with the R.E.M.E. badge, the other a badge of the 6th Guards Tank Brigade to which they were attached.
(Photo. via Tony Moor.)

Further publications containing Buzz Bomb material:-

BOOKS

Doodlebugs and Rockets	Bob Ogley	Froglet Press	1993
Front Line Folkestone		Folkestone Herald	1945
Kent Unconquered	H.R.Pratt-Boorman	Kent Messenger	1951
The Battle of the Flying Bomb	Bob Ogley	Froglet Press	1994
The Doodle Bugs	Norman Longmate	Heineman	1984
The Flying Bomb	Peter G. Cooksley	Robert Hale	1979
War on the Line	Bernard Darwin	Southern Railway	1946
A Third Kentish Patchwork	R.H.Goodsell	Stedhill	1970
Unexploded Bomb	A.B.Hartley	Cassell	1958
The Kent County Administration in War 1939 - 45	W.L. Platts	K.C.C	1946
Observer's Tale - The Story of Group 17 of the R.O.C		Roland Bros.	1950

BOOKLETS and PAMPHLETS

Air Operations by Air Defence of Great Britain and Fighter Command in Connection with the German Flying Bomb and Rocket Offensive 1944 - 45
Air Chief Marshal Sir Roderick Hill Supplement to the London Gazette,
Tuesday 19th October 1948

Balloons v Flying Bombs Air Vice Marshal W.C.C Gell
R.A.F Journal November 1944

Beccehamian - Magazine of the County School for Boys,
Beckenham and Penge Vol VI No.7 Summer Term 1945

Farningham against Hitler, Bernard Brew, Kentish District Times1946

In Bomb Alley E.S Oak-Rhind Local Government Service
Vol XXIII No 10 Oct 1944

NEWSPAPERS and MAGAZINES
(reports and articles in various issues)

The Aeroplane, Aeronautics, Aircraft Recognition, A.R.P and N.F.S Review, Broadstairs and St Peter's Mail, Folkestone, Hythe & District Herald, Isle of Thanet Gazette, Kentish District Times, Kent Messenger, Thanet Times.